A MINISTRY RENEWED

A Ministry Renewed

GORDON E. HARRIS

SCM PRESS LTD
LONDON

SBN 334 01013 6

First published 1968
by SCM Press Ltd
56 Bloomsbury Street London WC1

© SCM Press Ltd 1968

Printed in Great Britain by
Billing & Sons Limited
Guildford and London

To

Paul, Elizabeth, John and Michael

Children of the Manse

Contents

Acknowledgments

M y thanks are due to Dr Brian Lake of the Clinical Theology Association for kindly reading and commenting on the contents of Chapters 2 and 4.

I wish to thank my former colleagues on the team of the Presbyterian East London Training Centre for Industrial Evangelism for much valuable stimulus in the preparation of this book; also the members of John Knox Church, Stepney, for their forbearance during their minister's theological upheavals.

My thanks are also due to Mrs Rosemary Bugg for so patiently deciphering and typing the manuscript.

Finally, I wish to express my gratitude to my wife for her help and support during the period of personal mental and spiritual travail which led to the writing of this book.

Aston Tirrold   GORDON E. HARRIS
Berkshire

Introduction

T H E signs are out that we are reaching what can only be called the 'crisis of the local congregations'. At the seminary of a major denomination over 40% of the first year's students report that they do not desire to become ministers of a local congregation. It is reported further that there is a decline in students offering themselves for the ministry, and that many who could be expected to offer refuse to do so because they believe that to become the minister of a congregation does not place them at the point where the true frontier of the Christian mission is to be found.[1]

With these words Colin W. Williams begins his book *Where in the World?*, which he describes as 'a study of changing forms of the Church's witness'. This book and its sequel *What in the World?* offer a pithy and devastating analysis of the failures of the American congregational-centred Church to come to grips with a pluriform and secularized society. The situation of the Church in this country is little different in this respect from that of the American Church. The need for new ministries and new 'ecclesial forms', to use the current jargon, was never more evident than today. But, whether we like it or not, the local residential congregation is still the basic unit of the Church's structure. A great deal of manpower is still tied up in the institutional church as most of us know it. And it is with the men

[1] Colin W. Williams, *Where in the World?*, Epworth Press, 1965, pp. 1 f.

and women who comprise the ordained ministry of the main denominations that this book is primarily concerned. Dr Williams sees the problem mainly from the standpoint of the Church's structural defects. I wish to look at the problem from the standpoint of the men and women who must work within the present structures of the Church. Dr Williams refers to the number of students or potential students who give up the idea of ordination from the very start. He fails to mention the ministers already ordained who change to other professions in the middle of their careers. But even the statistics of departure from the full-time ordained ministry say nothing (*a*) of the ministers who labour on within it, having already lost their early vision and zeal, (*b*) of the ministers who have left the pastorate of the local congregation to take up work within the growing ecclesiastical bureaucracy and (*c*) of the ministers who from the day of their ordination have combined a part-time pastorate with the exercise of a full-time 'secular' calling.

This book is a very personal statement of the question : How best can we use the manpower already committed to the full-time paid service of the Church? I myself almost left the ministry of the Presbyterian Church of England after twelve years in its service. The pressures upon me to do this were manifold and complicated. One factor was a growing personal awareness of what the Gospel was saying (something I had lacked hitherto though I had tried to keep up the pretence of having it), combined with a feeling that I could no longer express this awareness within the structure of the Church as I knew it. In my own mind the terms 'Gospel' and 'Church' had become almost antithetical. This feeling had nothing to do with the generally rather facile separation of 'Gospel' and 'Church' which marks the average Englishman's view of Christianity. I did not wish to endorse the Gospel (even if that were possible) at the expense of endorsing the idea of a community which could be seen as a fruit of that Gospel. It was rather the contrast between that community as it might be and the Church as it now is that gave me the greatest frustration. It seemed content to carry on making the same claims for itself as it had always done without questioning their validity in any depth. This personal dissatisfaction with the Church as it was, compared with what it might be, was clinched for me by a television broadcast in the B.B.C. 'Viewpoint' series in which Albert H. van den Heuvel, the Youth Secretary of the World Council of Churches, spoke on the theme of the 'humiliation of the Church'. When asked what he meant by this phrase van den Heuvel replied:

First of all, I mean that the Church professes to be one thing, but it really is another. If you listen to what the Church pronounces itself to be and what it says about itself, then it always says that it is the institution which is unique in society because it, for instance, shows the unity of God; it's the only institution in society where people who do not normally meet can meet each other; classes are irrelevant, ages are irrelevant, men-women relationships are seen there in a very different perspective, the races, all, can assemble together in the Church. If you look at the actual situation of the Church, it doesn't show anything of that at all. It's a class-structure; it's mainly middle-class; it has fringes to the other side but not very much. It's certainly not united, not one at all, and it's not a unique institution in society but follows the society in which it lives very closely, to an extent that really it does not at all show up what it professes to be. Instead of being indeed a relevant institution in which people find a place where they are sharpened for their role in life, their relations with people, their involvement in politics and social affairs, you'll find a Church which is humiliated by the fact that it's largely irrelevant to modern people; it serves the religious life of people at a tiny little level on which people also exist, but it does not anywhere show the fullness of life which it always has said it did.

Van den Heuvel was then asked the reason for this failure. Was it because the Church hadn't caught up with the modern world?

It hasn't caught up, first of all with its own calling. And that is related to what you are asking, because if you see what the Church is, as far as I understand it, in the New Testament, and also in its best expressions through the ages (because there have always been small groups in the Church which have been very aware of that), then the Church says that it is like Jesus was in his time, a servant, or, if the Church is feminine, then it's a slave-girl in society; it watches the world change and in a changing world it is relevant to the people who are at that time living. Now what you see in the actual Church is that we always try to be faithful to our past, rather than to our present, that we have very little hope for the future. The Church . . . sees all the changes that come around it with great fear, but I think that it is . . . uniquely equipped for change. It has a freedom because guilt in the Church is forgiven and the future is open; we always expect new things from God who goes before us . . . but in actual fact there is very little to be seen of that. I think that's the main humiliation of the Church, as it would be the big humiliation of any living person, that it's a hypocrite—you say one thing and you don't do it![2]

These words of van den Heuvel spoke immediately to my condition and reinforced the strong sense I had that my vocation lay elsewhere than in the ministry. But there was another factor which prompted me at that time to offer myself for training as a professional social worker. It was anger both with myself and the Church. I was angry because for twelve years I also had suffered the humiliation of trying to be one thing when in reality I was another. I had always tried to be the model of what a minister should be and was expected to be. I had always tried to say and do the 'right thing', often at the expense of truthful and realistic dealings with my various congregations. I could do no other, for I had not yet found my identity as a man and was therefore looking to the ministry to supply me with the missing factor. My centre of gravity lay in other people's opinions of me

[2] Broadcast on 30th June 1965. See also van den Heuvel, *The Humiliation of the Church*, SCM Press, 1967, pp. 48 ff.

and the fantasy images of their own perfection which they projected on to me. The strain that this assumed role placed upon me eventually caused me to withdraw, emotionally and spiritually exhausted, from the arena for a few weeks. My anger on realizing the pressures to conformity which had moulded me for so long eventually erupted in the form of a move to leave the ministry. I was angry particularly on behalf of my long-suffering family, for they had been the scapegoats upon whom I had projected my frustration and inner rebellion. I was angry with myself, above all, for allowing myself to collude with this situation out of a desire to earn an acceptance with others that I felt I did not already possess.

The climax to this struggle with myself came when I wrote an article for our denominational magazine on the subject of prayer. The editorial headline 'Why I gave up prayer' was admittedly tendentious and misleading; for the article did not reject prayer as such but only a certain view of it. It seemed, however, that many of the readers never got beyond the headline before reaching for their pens in order to express their shock and displeasure at seeing a minister of the Church actually questioning the traditional modes of prayer. It is significant, however, that only one of the letters printed came from a minister; the rest were from laymen. The editor told me that three other ministers had written to express disagreement, although their letters were not printed. Three ministers had written to me privately expressing their views on the article (mainly in favour). In charity I could only assume that ministers failed to write because of their unwillingness to rebuke a colleague in public. But only two ministers expressed disagreement to me privately, either verbally or in writing. This silence seemed, and still seems, ominous. It reflected all too clearly the compliant, equivocal self whom I had unconsciously been attacking in the article and with whom I felt so angry. I had fully expected disagreement with my sentiments, but the silence was depressing. So I set the wheels in motion for my departure from the ministry.

Naturally, I had fully rationalized my course of action. My own theological views endorsed my plans. I would not, so I argued, have been leaving the ministry of the Church in any real sense of the word. As a layman I would have been as much a minister as the ordained minister himself, in fact more so, in so far as the ordained minister was there to train the church members for their own ministry in the world. But when it came to the point, I could not take the plunge into the 'secular' world.

The reasons for changing my mind were again manifold and complicated. Negatively speaking, I was aware that I was in bondage, financially speaking, to the pattern of life which I had adopted as a minister. The hazards of buying a house and living on a student's grant for a year were daunting in the extreme. It had been made almost impossible for me to start a new way of life by the very benevolence of the system of minimum stipend and rent-free housing (both of a fairly high standard) to which I and my family had become accustomed. I was virtually imprisoned within the structure from which I was struggling to break free. Positively speaking, however, I suddenly felt a renewed and deepened personal commitment to the ordained ministry as such. The experience of preparing a young family for the baptism of their child triggered off the counter-reaction. As long as men and women were still required to perform these services for people at the turning points of their lives—however misguided and ill-conceived their motives in asking for such services might appear to be—I was required to remain in the ordained ministry. I also felt a debt of gratitude to my denomination and its officials for their very real kindness to me at numerous points of crisis in my ministry, not least at the point where I threatened to leave it. For twelve years they had held me to them, threatening and exhausting though the relationship often was, in order to help me, quite simply, to grow up and assume a more mature responsibility for my actions as a minister of Word and Sacrament. For that, I could never cease to be grateful. I was also aware of a movement of thinking in the Church which required what little support and encouragement I could give it from within the situation. So I decided to stay.

The reader will, I trust, forgive these autobiographical remarks, but, in a sense, this whole book is autobiographical. The views on the ministry that I shall put forward have all been tested to a greater or lesser extent in my own ministry, particularly my ministry in the East End of London. No originality can be claimed for my views, which reflect much current thinking in the Church at all levels. The experience, however, of seeing this thinking come alive in practice prompts me to add one more volume to the growing corpus of writings on the subject of Church and Ministry today.

I

The Minister is a Man

DURING the last year or so I have come to know and understand more and more the profound this-worldliness of Christianity. The Christian is not a *homo religiosus*, but simply a
man, as Jesus was a man—in contrast, shall we say, to John the
Baptist. I don't mean the shallow and banal this-worldliness of
the enlightened, the busy, the comfortable, or the lascivious, but
the profound this-worldliness, characterized by discipline and
the constant knowledge of death and resurrection. I think Luther
lived a this-worldly life in this sense.

I remember a conversation that I had in America thirteen years
ago with a young French pastor. We were asking ourselves quite
simply what we wanted to do with our lives. He said he would
like to become a saint (and I think it is quite likely that he did
become one). At the time I was very impressed, but I disagreed
with him, and said, in effect, that I should like to learn to have
faith. For a long time I did not realize the depth of the contrast.
I thought I could acquire faith by trying to live a holy life, or
something like it. . . .

I discovered later, and I am still discovering right up to this
moment, that it is only by living completely in this world that
one learns to have faith. One must completely abandon any
attempt to make something of oneself, whether it be a saint, or a
converted sinner, or a churchman (a so-called priestly type!), a
righteous man or an unrighteous one, a sick man or a healthy
one. By this-worldliness I mean living unreservedly in life's
duties, problems, successes and failures, experiences and perplexi-
ties. In so doing we throw ourselves completely into the arms of
God, taking seriously, not our own sufferings, but those of God
in the world—watching with Christ in Gethsemane. That, I

think, is faith, that is *metanoia*; and that is how one becomes a
man and a Christian (cf. Jer. 45!). How can success make us
arrogant, or failure lead us astray, when we share in God's
sufferings through a life of this kind?[1]

'Bonhoeffer with everything' would seem to be the recipe for
every budding theologian these days. Ever since the Bishop of
Woolwich first brought him to the notice of the British public,
the name of the German theologian-martyr has been both a
rallying-cry for the 'new' and anathema to the 'old' theologians.
My only reason for quoting him is that, like so many recent
writers, he asks the right questions about what it means to be a
Christian. To the younger generation of ministers, particularly,
his words have the fresh air of reality blowing through them.
They point to the basic calling of any minister, to be a human
being.

Had I headed this chapter 'The minister *as* a man' I would
have been suggesting that the minister's humanity was only one
component in the total structure of his ministry. This is far from
the case. The *only* thing that the minister has to give to his
fellows is his humanity. And it is precisely that which the
Church in its present form most hinders him from giving. Much
of the rest of this book will be concerned with the details of how
a minister can offer his humanity to the world. For the present
we must explore further the proposition that to be a Christian
means to be simply a human being.

Dietrich Bonhoeffer's thinking has a distinguished ancestry.
Basically it springs from the New Testament itself, as we shall
see later in this chapter. But the nineteenth-century Danish
thinker, Kierkegaard, said the same thing in his exquisite picture of the 'Knight of Faith' in his book *Fear and Trembling*.
The passage should be read as a whole to gain the real flavour
of it, but here is an extract:

[1] Dietrich Bonhoeffer, *Letters and Papers from Prison*, SCM Press, Re-
vised Edition 1967, pp. 201-2.

I have never discovered a knight of faith, but I can easily imagine one. Here he is. I make his acquaintance, I am introduced to him. And the moment I lay eyes on him, I push him away and leap back suddenly, clap my hands together and say half aloud : 'Good God! Is this really he? Why, he looks like an Inspector of Taxes!' But it is really he. I draw closer to him. I watch every movement he makes to see whether he shows any sign of the least telegraphic communication with the infinite, a glance, a look, a gesture, an air of melancholy, a smile to betray the contrast of infinity and the finite. But no! I examine him from head to foot, hoping to discover a chink through which the infinite can peer through. But no! He is completely solid. How does he walk? Firmly. He belongs wholly to the finite; and there is no townsman dressed in his Sunday best, who spends his Sunday afternoon in Frederiksberg who treads the earth more firmly than he; he belongs altogether to the earth, no bourgeois more so.[2]

If a minister is to remind other people of their true humanity, he must first be led to discover his own for himself. Any training for the ministry should involve the same kind of disciplined growth into self-awareness as is required, say, of a social case-worker. But I see as yet little acceptance in theological training circles of the need for helping an ordinand to know and accept himself wholly as a human being. Even a document as forward-looking as *The Shape of the Ministry*, drawn up by a working party set up by the British Council of Churches,[3] gives scant attention to the need for helping a man to develop emotionally as well as intellectually for what is, after all, one of the most emotionally demanding professions in the world. In its recommendations on the training of presbyters (pp. 50 ff.) six pages are devoted to intellectual training in the various theological disciplines and just over one page to training in coping with personal relationships (this under the heading of 'other subjects').

[2] S. Kierkegaard, *Fear and Trembling*, trans. Robert Payne, Oxford University Press, 1939, p. 48.
[3] *The Shape of the Ministry*, British Council of Churches, 1965.

This is not to decry the need for a thorough intellectual ground-
ing in the faith. More, not less, is needed in these days of a
general rise in educational standards. But I am convinced that
people often grow *intellectually* as a consequence of being
allowed to develop *emotionally*. In fairness to the B.C.C. working party I must point out that its recommendations on alternative courses of training for men not academically inclined are
much more cognizant of modern research into the learning process than those on academic training for the ministry (pp. 56-68).
But even these fall far short of the kind of demands upon a man
to 'know himself' made of trainees for the other 'helping professions'.

I can speak on this from personal experience. I left my theological college after six years at university and one year as tutor in
my college. Intellectually I was reasonably well qualified to cope
with the normal demands of a Presbyterian preaching and teaching ministry. But emotionally I was still a babe-in-arms. Certainly
the experience of living in a residential college community had
knocked some of the rough edges off me. But the Christian faith
and the study of theology only came alive for me after the
experience of joining a seminar organized by the Clinical
Theology Association and receiving a scientifically-grounded
training in the basic patterns of human personality. The experience knocked me sideways for a while, but I can now never cease
to be grateful for the opportunity of learning to accept myself as
a man in both the acknowledged and hitherto unacknowledged
areas of my personality.

Many ministers reach this point without technical aids of any
kind. But since emotional growth is most subject to unconscious
resistance from within the human psyche, such growth should be
furthered by as keen a dedication to scientific expertise as we
bring to the study of the Scriptures. The Church can ill afford
to neglect any available means of assisting its ministers in the
eliciting of their humanity, for the minister is there to remind

people of their humanity. The average man, however, does not view the minister as a typical example of humanity. The figure of the stage parson is still not far from the truth about the clergy as a professional group. Of course, genuine humanity in a minister will always be ignored or misunderstood to the extent that the onlooker resists the lure of true humanity. But such misunderstanding is not what I refer to here. I refer to the sheer religiosity and failure to see life and people as interesting in themselves that mark so many ministers and the lay people they represent. To use people and situations as means to an end, be it to fill pews or save souls or in any other sense to shape the unshapeable into some preconceived metaphysical pattern, is to ignore humanity in our neighbour and to dehumanize ourselves. It took me ten years of my ministry to realize the truth of that fact. The shock of entering upon a ministry in the East End of London and finding how few people had any interest in the Church was traumatic. The breakthrough into a new outlook came when I realized that I had everything in common with those who regarded me as a visitor from Mars. Our humanity bound us together. Jesus, in his perfect humanity, declared all men accepted by God whether they acknowledged this acceptance or not. The only difference between a Christian and a non-Christian is that a Christian is supposed to have recognized and responded to this acceptance in terms of his own heightened humanity, while a non-Christian has not so recognized and responded to the divine acceptance. In principle the terms 'Christian' and 'human' should be identical. It is a tragedy that our ministerial preoccupation with people as potential 'Christians' has obscured the prior claim of the realization of their true humanity and has debased the term 'Christian' into a cliché no longer expressive of the reality it was intended originally to convey.

It is here that the role of the minister as a human being becomes paramount. In his book *The Gift of Ministry*, Daniel

Jenkins writes on the minister's vocation to be a representative man :

The purpose of the minister in the human economy is that he is set apart to be more or less 'full-time' what other men are able to be only occasionally, a representative man.

Now it is vital to understand the precise sense in which this is true. It is not suggested that the ministry must therefore be set apart as a special spiritual caste, an aristocracy of priesthood, with privileges and a dignity which do not belong to other men. On the contrary, to understand the minister as representative in the right sense is the one effective safeguard against that happening. For it reminds the minister that, from one side, the whole justification for his office consists in his being like other men, existing alongside them, sharing the same lot, knowing the same difficulties and doubts and temptations and comforts and hopes, trying to apprehend as a unity that common human nature which other men may apprehend only fragmentarily and confusedly, but often much more intensely and richly than he himself does.[4]

More recently the journalist Monica Furlong has pleaded for a similar view of the minister's role, though in more direct terms. In an article on 'The Parson's Role Today', published in *New Christian*, she states as one of her conclusions that 'the clergyman's role is to decrease his activity, to live much more in a state of being than in a state of doing. I don't underestimate just how difficult this is to practise; I only want to say that to this one layman the clergy who help and impress most are those who live in a state that is neither laziness nor hyper-activity.'

Miss Furlong writes against the familiar background of a society in which people are becoming more and more isolated from each other emotionally and mentally if not physically. As she says :

In England in 1966 we see a great emphasis upon security—the security, that is, that is offered by affluence and a Welfare

[4] D. Jenkins, *The Gift of Ministry*, Faber and Faber, 1947, p. 60.

State. There is great emphasis upon success and on status—it is important to be in the right job—a job which carries prestige. It is important to be insulated against suffering of any kind—an attitude that is easy to sympathize with and to some extent to share, but it also begins, I suspect, to be important to be insulated against having to have close contact with other human beings, and if I am right in my diagnosis, then this may be evidence of a schizoid tendency within our whole society.[5]

This increasing anonymity of present-day society has of course its positive aspects. In our densely populated urban communities it is necessary up to a point to be anonymous and insulated from one's immediate neighbours if one is to remain human at all. Nevertheless, the ability to benefit from the anonymity of modern urban society demands a high degree of maturity and responsibility in the new city dwellers. In the absence of these things the loneliness and isolation of which Monica Furlong writes become all too common. It is here that I see the relevance of her plea that clergymen should witness to the importance of being rather than doing. This witness is a function of the whole Church, not of ministers only. The demonic aspects of anonymity can only be exorcized through the embodiment in the life of the Church of the insight that ultimately people are ends in themselves, not means to an end. The Christian awareness of the sanctity of the personality must extend to wholehearted resistance against the contemporary pressure upon individuals to withdraw entirely into their own shells. This withdrawal is often accompanied by frantic attempts to justify their own existence in terms of status-seeking activity which leaves them little freedom to be human.

Unfortunately the churches have tended to succumb to a similar activism. The Free Churches in England have perhaps succumbed more than most. The norm of church life still tends to be the busy organization-church, with the minister playing

[5] M. Furlong, 'The Parson's Role Today', *New Christian*, 16th June 1966, p. 12.

the role of business manager. Even the annual statistical schedule of membership and finance required of congregations by denominational headquarters symbolizes, for me at least, the false criteria on which we base the success of the Church. In an age when they have been shorn of almost all their traditional social status ministers are especially prone to become activistic and bent on self-justification. I am still appalled at the extent to which ministers, of whom I am one, tend when gathered together to ply each other with tales of their achievements and successes. It is so unnecessary, for it is not by these that the Church is ultimately judged. The ultimate measure of the Church's success is the extent to which it has restored men and women to themselves and thus to God. This it does by mediating to them the awareness that they are accepted for what they are, not for what they can achieve. Achievement is not ruled out of this pattern but takes its proper place as the expression of joy at the awareness of one's status as an accepted and loved person and not as the means to gaining that status. Achievement in the former sense is always spontaneous and free. Achievement in the latter sense is always slavish and grudging, since it is performed out of fear of the consequences.

It is impressive to see the extent to which modern trends in industry bear out this profound Christian insight into the relationship between status and achievement. Automation in factories and increasingly in offices is reducing the effort of daily work to the minimum. Men are gradually being set free from the necessity of doing what machines do more easily and effectively. Modern industry requires an ever smaller labour force as the machine takes over from man. Full employment will in future be seen in terms other than those dictated by the requirement that every man should have a 'job' in order to reap the benefits of the economy. We shall, in fact, have to pay people to do what they like!

In this connection I think of the bus-conductress featured in a recent television programme on the lives of the inhabitants of a certain London square. For her the drudgery of bus-conducting was simply the means by which she was set free to do what she most loved—sculpture. Her sculpture was her life. Through it she was placing her humanity and integrity as a person at the disposal of her fellows. She lived by being rather than doing.

Here I have been helped by my experience as a minister in the East End of London. One advantage of being in a situation where the Church has failed in the traditional sense is that one is set free to ask the right questions about what it means to be the Church. It is not a rationalization of failure to say that in the East End the importance of being rather than doing becomes paramount. True achievement and maturity flow from an experience of being accepted and loved for one's own sake as a son or daughter of God. When people see Christians as being simply there for them, refusing to manipulate or cajole them into any preconceived pattern of allegiance or behaviour, then they will feel free to take seriously the Gospel of a love which desires only that people should be themselves. Such love is expressed only in the lives of people who have learnt the art of being rather than doing. The minister above all must have learned this art if he is to begin setting others free to be human themselves. The obstacles, however, in the way of this ministry of liberation are enormous, as we shall see when we turn in the next chapter to a scrutiny of patterns of congregational life.

2

Minister and Congregation

M U C H criticism of the Church today centres upon the 'minister-centredness' of local congregations. The rightful emphasis that is currently being placed upon the layman as the spearhead of the Church's mission and the minister as helping to prepare him for that mission marks a healthy reaction from the clericalism which infects all the main denominations, not least the Presbyterian. We Presbyterians tend to pride ourselves upon the democracy of our church government, dependent as it is upon the joint co-operation of laymen, known as 'elders', who are elected by the congregation, and the minister whom we dignify as 'first among equals'. But discerning observers of the workings of our ecclesiastical machinery have pointed out that in reality Presbyterianism is an oligarchy, comprised of an often self-perpetuating church session (the English Presbyterian 'Book of Order' allows for nomination by the session of candidates for the eldership) and a minister whose security of tenure is hardly less firm than that offered to the Anglican incumbent by the 'parson's freehold'.

The situation has been analysed in that influential book, *God's Frozen People*, by Mark Gibbs and T. Ralph Morton, who declare:

The new conception of the minister as the little king of a little kingdom is an affront to the faith and the intelligence of the members of the Church and a constant frustration to individuals and groups in the Church who want to be more active in their obedience and even to make experiments. The layman comes to feel that the Church is ruled by the clergy and that the exercise of his gifts is not to be encouraged.

The authors go on to point out that many members of the congregation prefer things to be this way :

They have been brought up to see their Church membership in terms of their relationship to the minister; not in terms of their relationship to their fellow-members. 'I go to Father Black's mass.' 'Pastor White baptized me.' Status in the local church is often in terms of this relationship. One of the reasons why a church likes an 'attentive minister' and the reason why a visit from a curate is not very highly regarded is this matter of status. So the 'loyal' part of the congregation likes and upholds the centrality of the minister. And however much a minister may strive for other things, he yet likes to feel that he is appreciated. He has lost a great deal of the position he used to have in the community—in his own right as a leader of society. Now, when he has sunk into a social equality with others, he is apt to find the justification of his position in the dependence of others upon him.[1]

It is surprising that where the consequences of such clericalism are deemed to be so serious a great deal more profound study of the situation is not pursued. Mere exhortations to abolish the 'clergy-line' will have little effect unless we ask ourselves : Why is the traditional dependence upon the minister so deep-rooted in our church-life and so resistant to surgery? Mark Gibbs and Ralph Morton hint at an answer to these questions when they suggest unconscious factors at work in the situation. A survey of some of these deeper factors determining the relationship between minister and congregation must yield valuable pointers to the means by which the true humanity of the minister may be made freely available to his fellow-members of the Church in the

[1] M. Gibbs and T. R. Morton, *God's Frozen People*, Fontana Books, Collins, 1964, pp. 50 f.

interests of their true humanity and ultimately of the world itself.

The source of insight for such a survey is provided by modern research into 'group dynamics' or 'group interaction'. The results of such research are gradually being applied to the work of the Church. The rediscovery of the Church as the 'therapeutic community' is bound up with the rediscovery of the importance of small 'face-to-face' groups in assisting the growth of church members to maturity. The traditional relationship of minister and congregation still constitutes, however, one of the greatest obstacles to growth. The blame for this situation cannot be laid at the door of the clergy or the laity separately. It is the result of collusion between the infantile dependency needs of both minister and congregation. Such collusion is, by definition, unconscious. Without insight into the nature of it neither ministers nor lay-people will be able to shake free of a relationship which is highly resistant to treatment.

Basic to this situation is the phenomenon of the 'transference'. It is a common fallacy to suppose that the phenomenon of transference is confined to the psycho-analyst's consulting room. It affects all our every-day relationships. None of us sees our neighbours as they really are. Our impressions of them are always distorted to the extent that we transfer to them these imperfectly repressed feelings about the important figures in our early infancy whom these neighbours in some way typify or symbolize. This explains why people can arouse in us the most powerful feelings of love or hate in a way barely commensurate with the length of our acquaintance with them. The 'first impressions' that we regard as so important in our assessment of other people, and the phenomenon of 'love at first sight' are only explicable as the result of the triggering-off of feelings already latent in our minds.

The transference is an inescapable element in the relationship between minister and congregation. Any authoritarian figure such as a minister is capable of arousing the strongest feelings of love and hate in the persons who are in any measure dependent upon him. It is important, then, that a minister should receive some basic training in the workings of groups and some understanding of the phenomenon of the transference. Without this training he will be rendered unduly anxious by the strongly ambivalent feelings of love and hatred which members of his congregation will transfer upon him. The early years of my ministry were marred for me quite unnecessarily by my ignorance of the transference situation. Many a night I barely slept for agonizing over some hurtful or cutting remark made by a church member. The agonies I suffered had little real relationship to the extent of my genuine failures in obligation towards my congregation. Genuine guilt, frankly acknowledged and healthily accepted, is never a cause of sleeplessness to any minister. What does bother him is the threat to his security and well-being posed by the exciting of his own guilt-feelings as a result of the projection upon him of the guilt-feelings of others. Here I must point out that the term 'projection' has a slightly different meaning from that of 'the transference'. 'The transference' describes the process of transferring feelings about significant people in one's early life upon people in later life who stand in an analogous relationship to us. 'Projection' describes the process of imputing others with the guilt aroused by aspects of our personality which we cannot acknowledge even to ourselves. Such projection is a means of attacking our own guilt without, paradoxically, suffering the pain of feeling guilty ourselves. The things we cannot tolerate in ourselves are the things we cannot tolerate in others. The minister is often the object of just this kind of projected guilt as he is of the transferred feelings to which I earlier referred. Awareness of what is happening can be used by the minister constructively in his pastoral work, as we shall see in Chapter 4. Ignorance of what is happening simply cripples the minister and unfits him for effective action.

Here we need to sketch briefly four main types of personality pattern and the related transference situations to which they tend to give rise. But a warning must first be made regarding the danger of dismissing people as 'types'. There is no better way of keeping others at a distance than by isolating one factor in their personality and postulating it as the whole truth about them. This is a refined way of 'giving a dog a bad name and hanging him'. People are a mixture of different emotional responses covering the whole spectrum of personality. The label we apply is only a very rough and ready indication of the preponderant element in a person's emotional make-up. Any failure to see the whole person as a human being in his own right would be the height of immaturity on the part of the minister. Yet some understanding of personality types is necessary if the minister's pastoral functions are to be exercised with any degree of precision.

The *hysterical* personality is well known to every minister. This type of person, usually, though by no means always, a woman, is noted for the tendency to over-identify herself with other people, particularly in this case the minister. Every conceivable opportunity is taken to compel the minister to take notice of her. This attention-seeking behaviour usually results in the isolation of the hysterical person as a result of the dislike and jealousy she arouses in others. Basic to this personality pattern is the repressed panic at the possibility of being left unattended and unnoticed. The panic stems from the period in early infancy when the baby was compelled to force mother to take notice of her because of an apparent lack of attention on her part. An absence or poverty of relationship with father also contributes significantly to the development of the hysterical personality. In fact, in relation to the hysteric, the question I often ask myself regarding which parent he or she is in fantasy seeking, almost always produces the answer, 'Father!'. The pattern of attention-seeking behaviour becomes built into the growing personality and repeats itself in relation to the parent-figures who crop up in adult life. The hysterical woman tends to be the bane of every minister, and not only ministers! The frivolous distinction between a good psychiatrist and a brilliant psychiatrist contains a great deal of truth: the good psychiatrist recognizes an hysteric when he sees one, the brilliant psychiatrist runs away faster! Hysterical people are adept at arousing panic in others, and the very demandingness of their behaviour tends to exhaust the emotional resources of their helpers very quickly. Occasionally the hysterical woman succeeds in exciting the collusion of the minister, with the result that yet another story of 'Vicar runs off with organist's wife' appears in the *News of the World*.

A second familiar personality type is the *paranoid*. This kind of person is noted for the tendency to feel easily persecuted. He tends to be aggressive in manner and to throw his weight around in committee meetings. He is the 'awkward cuss' who will upset the carefully laid plans of the most responsible decision-making body. Basic to this personality is the feeling that everybody is hostile to him. This feeling has its roots in the situation in infancy when mother suddenly withdraws the wholehearted attention which she hitherto has lavished freely upon her young child, possibly upon the arrival of a baby brother or sister. From being the loving provider mother suddenly becomes, in the eyes of the child, a persecutor. The deeply repressed feeling of loathsomeness associated with this situation is projected upon other people in later life. The 'paranoid' person desperately needs love. But even loving attention on the part of others has a persecutory quality about it. Therefore he must make others hate him, in order to confirm this picture of himself as hateful. Every minister will have at least one such person in his congregation.

A third personality type is the *depressive*. The depressive person generally sees the minister as a man to be placated. His

B

deeply repressed rage against the original mother-figure becomes overlaid by the neurotic guilt aroused by the very destructiveness of his feelings. As a compensation he idealizes mother and adopts a pattern of compliant behaviour which is the very antithesis of his real feelings. He tends, therefore, to be strict and conventional in his church practice and ever-willing to help with the meanest of chores. There is little joy in his religious profession, which bears more of the marks of Law than of Gospel. This would explain the situation so fascinatingly described by the American theologian Gibson Winter in his book *The Suburban Captivity of the Churches*. He writes:

It is possible that organizational activities provide some members with a means to work out feelings of guilt through sacrifices of time and energy in organizational drudgery. This interpretation explains the 'drive' behind much of the activity. Although members often complain about the drudgery, they not only do it but seem to need it as well. Their cherished Sunday mornings are devoted to one semi-religious activity or another as a way of atoning for guilt feelings through sacrificial behaviour.

The idea of atoning for guilt through organizational drudgery suggests that the activities of the churches provide a Protestant system of penance. Members do penance for their faults by sharing in the organizational work. . . . Cooking a supper or serving on a committee may seem far removed from repeating the Hail Mary, but organizational drudgery does seem to fulfil a similar function in the metropolitan congregation; members atone for their guilt by performing unpleasant tasks for the organization; to this extent the organizational network becomes a secularized penitential system and *the pastor who solicits their labours becomes the punishing father*.[2]

The support for this unconscious penitential system most naturally comes from the more depressive members of the congregation, whose efforts tend to be directed at earning a status

---

[2] Gibson Winter, *The Suburban Captivity of the Churches*, Doubleday and Co., 1961, pp. 96 f.

which deep down they feel they can never receive as the free gift it ought to be and is, according to the Gospel.

A fourth personality type is the so-called *schizoid*. This kind of person betrays opposite characteristics to the 'hysteric'. If the hysterical person tends to seek his security in attachment to people, the schizoid person tends to seek his security in detachment from people. He can be the typical 'cold fish', a description which is as uncharitable as it is incorrect. The schizoid person's apparent emotional detachment masks a very deep hunger for relationships. Such a hunger was first aroused by a felt lack of 'mothering' in early infancy. So stressed is the infant in these circumstances that he suffers a revulsion of feeling against emotional attachments of any kind. This revulsion has a triple source, first, in the feeling that, were the sufferer to make any emotional demands on others at all they would become overweening demands, so deep is the repressed emotional hunger; second, in the feeling that to expose oneself to personal relationships at all is to run the risk of opening old wounds and reliving the original infantile experience of dread and desolation; third, in the fear of being engulfed emotionally by the more hysterical and outgoing personalities. On all counts the schizoid individual avoids deep personal encounter with anybody.

This kind of person is very hard to pin down to active commitment to the Church. He often attends church regularly until the point where he is asked (in the Free Churches anyway) to become a member of the congregation; then he disappears. He is often the first to leave after the service and avoids the minister's handshake like the plague. Like the paranoid person, he can often give an impression of hostility towards others; in any event he tends to be unflattering in his attitude to other people. Yet the schizoid person rarely presents a picture of monolithic aversion to human relationships. His personality pattern usually combines both hysterical and schizoid components to the extent that hysterical attachment to some types of people co-exist with schizoid detachment from other types of people. Thus an hysterical attachment to mother-figures is often manifest in people who have a schizoid detachment from father-figures and vice versa.

This survey of four types of personality pattern must of necessity be sketchy, for this is not a book on pastoral psychology. My sole purpose in mentioning them in even this detail is to make clear some of the facts on which I base my plea for a more thorough training for the ministry. Such training must involve some knowledge of what makes groups, as well as individuals, tick. The transference situation can be a source of great anxiety to a minister if he is not equipped to recognize it, nor to make the necessary corrections for the complementary phenomenon of counter-transference. This is the situation in which he too transfers his own repressed hatreds, hungers and longings towards the members of his congregation. The hysterical person will tend to arouse panic in him to the extent that he is made to feel robbed of attention and emotionally drained by the overpowering demands of the parishioner. The paranoid person will make the minister feel persecuted and stimulate him to counter-attack. The depressive person will quickly activate the minister's own neurotic guilt feelings and the schizoid person will cause the minister to withdraw from pastoral involvement with him. The counter-transference situation arises as the result of what is termed 'collusion' between the unconscious needs of the minister and his congregation. Any effective pastoral work in this situation must be vitiated by the minister's inability to see just what people are doing to him. It is all the more easy, then, for the minister to be manipulated into playing a role in deference to the congregation's projected fantasies. He senses that he is being asked to do and be the wrong thing, but can do little about it.

Of course, no relationships between a minister and his congregation, however mature, will be devoid of aspects of infantile dependence. This dependence can be quite mutual and is perpetuated by the very system of clerical domination of which recent writers justifiably complain. The very desire on the minister's part to dominate and be the lynch-pin of the congregation's life is expressive of his own infantile dependence upon the attention and subservience of the congregation. At the same time, as the parent-figure in the set-up, he will inevitably have transferred to him the same demands as members of the congregation originally made of their own parents, i.e. to the same extent that these demands were never satisfied or were totally rejected. When the minister is able to recognize the aspects of infantile dependence on both sides of the relationship with his congregation he can begin to work towards a more mature and creative role both for himself and the church members. This will not be easy without technical aids to insight on behalf of both. When the minister is under pressure, for example, to satisfy his own neurotic ideal of perfection, he will readily succumb to the demand of the congregation that he be a 'good visitor'. Even if he recognizes this demand to be infantile, especially when he is known to be readily available to people in cases of real need, he will continue to feel guilty about his inability to fulfil this role. We are all adept at twisting other people's arms when we want them to do as we wish, and guilt-arousal is an almost infallible technique to that end.

Let us be clear about the problem we are trying to solve here. We are not discussing whether or not the minister should not be a leader within his congregation. The question concerns the *nature* of that leadership. Any group brought together for whatever purpose will look automatically for a leader. This fact was demonstrated by the War Office Selection Boards set up during the war to aid selection of candidates.

The W.O.S.B. submitted candidates to various problems and social stresses in an experimental micro-community of about eight members. The group was expected to perform tasks of different types, such as group discussions, physical and outdoor or indoor situations which necessitated some degree of collective planning. No leader was appointed since the intention was that the group should throw up its own natural leaders. . . . When we say that the group selected its leaders, we do not mean to imply that this was done by a show of hands or in any formal sense; the group was kept under observation while the collective tasks were being carried out and it was noted which men were spontaneously followed by the group in the varying situations which it had to face.[3]

The *kind* of leader any group will produce depends upon the degree of balance and maturity present within the members of the group. A sick community will throw up sick leaders, as did Hitler's Germany, for example. A 'sick' leader will, in turn, confirm the group in its own 'sickness'. If the minister is compulsively dependent upon having weak people around him, the possibilities for growth to maturity within the group will be stultified. Even where there is a great deal of negative transference in the congregation's attitude to the minister, i.e. when they are on bad terms with each other, their very mutual hatred sometimes binds them together and makes it very difficult for the relationship to be severed. This situation is analogous to the ill-treated child's often excessive emotional dependence upon a bad parent.

Recognition of the problems of creating healthy leadership within the Church is a necessary first step towards meeting the plea for the abolition of clerical domination. Clerical domination is never the result of the simple desire on the minister's part to be domineering, but the result also of the congregation's desire to be domineered. Unfortunately, part of the attraction of the ministry as a profession lies in the scope it gives for the very 'lording it over the flock' which our Lord condemned (Luke 22.25-27). One of the best correctives to the desire to be a 'little pope' is the experience of serving in a team ministry, where one

[3] J. A. C. Brown, *The Social Psychology of Industry*, Penguin Books, 1954, p. 243.

is subject to the scrutiny and criticism of one's peers. My own move from an individualistic ministry to a team ministry in the East End of London revealed both the extent of my individualism and the powerful effects of rivalry in my relationship with my colleagues. Like many ministers, I have always suffered the problem of coping with my jealousy of my fellow ministers. This began when I left the theological college and faced the continual temptation to compare my performance with that of college contemporaries. In my case the problem was aggravated by the fact that I was a twin, brought up in the more than usually provoking situation of having to share everything, including birthdays, with my twin sister. It was quite easy to see eventually how much my jealousy of colleagues was a projection of my jealousy of my twin, and how this in itself predisposed me to take up the individualistic occupation of a minister.

How far the individualism of the minister is allowed to distort the balance of a congregation's life depends to a great extent upon the structure of the congregation itself. The hierarchical structure of the Roman Catholic and Anglican Churches might appear to offer greater risk of 'lording it over the flock' on the part of the clergy. But my experience of the Free Churches testifies to the equal risk of clerical domination attaching to a system of church government which, negatively speaking, fails to check a clericalism which is the more insidious for being unacknowledged. The first step, therefore, towards the breakdown of clerical domination will be the achieving of insight into what personal relationships within a group do to people. No amount of theologizing about the Church as the 'laos of God', with the minister as himself one of the laity, existing to train his fellow-laity for witness, will cut any ice unless there is awareness of the deep unconscious factors which create the fatal collusion between the ecclesiastical 'prima donna' and his submissive followers. Only so will the relationship between minister and congregation cease to be one of mutual projection, and the minister's true humanity as a person in his own right begin to shine through the masks which he assumes or is forced to assume by others. Only then will he be set free to perform his true role—that of the *prophet*. To this role we shall now turn.

3

The Prophet

THIS book is deliberately one-sided in that it deals primarily with the ordained minister's role in the Church and the world. Such one-sidedness must inevitably obscure the fact that anything which can be said of the minister's role must be said of the role of the whole Church in society. The minister exists to point the Church to its true task, namely, to proclaim the 'mighty acts of God' to the world in which it is set. But the Church will always seek to escape this responsibility in so far as such proclamation sets up an almost intolerable tension between the Church and the world, and within the Church itself. If the Church is to proclaim the Gospel it must live by the Gospel. This is not so easy as it sounds. For the Gospel stands for ferment, for renewal, for growth and for change. Above all, it stands for openness to the future and freedom from bondage to the past. This is the only way I can interpret the death and resurrection of Jesus Christ. All the New Testament images of salvation imply the destruction of an old existence and the creation of a new one. Christianity is a revolutionary movement and Jesus was the Revolutionary *par excellence*.

But the last thing the Church, as an institution, wants to do is to change. Because it is composed of human beings, subject to all the frailties of their unregenerate humanity, it falls prey to the paralysis induced by acquiescence in unexamined attitudes and structures. This is why I pleaded in the last chapter for a closer scrutiny of patterns of congregational life. I do not regard psychological insights as the sole key to a renewed ministry. But I do regard them as one of the God-sent tools for enabling the Church to understand more fully the situation to which it is seeking to address itself. The minister's responsibility is to help the Church to understand the nature of its own prophetic calling and to exercise it. For that to happen, the minister must himself be a prophet.

It is customary to distinguish between the minister's prophetic and priestly functions and grant them equal status. I believe that this is a false antithesis. The basic Christian task is a prophetic one, i.e. to declare the truth about God's purpose for mankind as summed up in the story of the Man, Jesus of Nazareth. The prophetic word can be spoken in all kinds of ways, not least by those actions of the minister which we term 'priestly' or 'pastoral'. *Any* embodiment in a human life of God's attitude of unqualified acceptance of man is a prophetic act, reflecting that supremely prophetic act, the Incarnation itself. The prophetic ministry is therefore the basic ministry, in the light of which all the priestly functions of the minister are to be seen and judged.

This statement deserves elaboration, for it is far too commonly thought that a minister cannot exercise both a prophetic and priestly ministry. It is true that a minister who is given to much fulminating on current issues from the pulpit tends to be less well-equipped for the pastoral role. It is also common for church people to shake their heads and say, 'our minister is a good pastor but a rotten preacher'. But preaching is only a part of prophecy and not the major part either. The Old Testament prophets often conveyed their message by symbolic actions as well as by words (cf. Ezek. 3.24-5.4). Any word or action is prophetic when it demonstrates the truth about God's relationship to man. We must be able to ask of any of the minister's (and, by implication, the Church's) words and actions: What is their prophetic content? Do they carry the authority which derives from their reflecting the truth of the Gospel? Or how far are they empty words and empty actions to the extent that they pervert the truth of the Gospel or are devoid of it? Such questions are not easily answered except in terms of an evaluation of the elements in a truly prophetic ministry.

A prophetic ministry, as I understand it, is first and foremost a listening ministry. It is no coincidence that the Old Testament prophets were men whose ears were finely tuned to the sounds of the world in which they lived. To change the metaphor abruptly, they kept their finger on the pulse of society. They also reflected deeply upon the word that they felt God was calling them to speak to their society.

A second feature of the prophetic ministry is that it is a responsible ministry. It sees itself as inextricably involved with the whole life of mankind and not merely with the so-called 'religious' dimension. The burden of the Hebrew prophets' attack upon burnt offerings and sacrifices was not that these things in themselves were wrong but that they were pursued in irresponsible forgetfulness of the total life of man, his physical as well as his spiritual needs (cf. Isa. 58).

A third feature of the prophetic ministry is that it submits itself continually to the judgment of its own message. In other words, it remains continually alive to the dangers of hypocrisy.

A fourth feature of the prophetic ministry is that it is detached. This is not a contradiction of its role of total involvement in the society to which it is addressing itself. The true prophet, however, recognizes the boundaries between the world and himself, and avoids the risk either of over-identifying himself with the situation he is confronting or of taking flight from it in a selfish preoccupation with 'religious' concerns.

This is a far from exhaustive summary of the nature of the prophetic ministry, but it does provide us with a yardstick by which we can measure the validity of much that is carried on in the name of Christian ministry today. Most of this chapter will centre on the 'listening' role of the prophet, for it is from here that I believe the basic failure in prophecy today springs.

As regards the listening role of the prophet, I detect today a greater readiness of ministers to listen to what is going on in the world before they begin to open their mouths. But the trend has by no means gone far enough. There is still far too much resistance to the plain facts about the condition of man, nature and society which enquirers in all disciplines are revealing to us. I have already referred to one obvious example of such resistance, namely that shown towards psychological insights of all kinds. Such resistance can easily be explained in terms of the anxiety which the probing of areas of repressed mental pain arouse in us all. But let me point out here that psychology has as its first concern the discerning of 'truth in the inward parts' (Ps. 51.6). In face of the impressive testimonies from the field of psycho-therapy to the freedom which discernment of this truth, however unpalatable, has brought to countless sufferers, it ill behoves the Church to stop its ears to what psychology is saying about the true aspect of man's inner being.

Another field of enquiry for which the Church's ears need to be sharpened is the field of sociology. Such little examination as has been made of the question of sociological factors affecting Church allegiance has proved beyond a shadow of doubt that history and geography play a large part in the failure of the Church's mission to present-day society. F. Boulard's fascinating book, *An Introduction to Religious Sociology*, makes quite clear how the churchgoing habits of whole areas in France have been determined by the nature of its terrain and its communications. He traces, for example, a chain of weak religious practice coinciding with a geological fault crossing Brittany and finishing in the Bocage of Normandy. 'It is formed of parishes where there are quarries. Granite quarries and dechristianization go to-

gether.'[1] This blunt statement carries a whole world of meaning.
As a minister in a working-class community I also had my eyes
opened by reading E. R. Wickham's book, *Church and People in
an Industrial City*.[2] I was staggered to discover that working-
class people do not go to church partly because the Church for
several centuries excluded them by providing very few seats in
the churches for them. Up to the middle of the nineteenth century the pews were mainly rented by members of the upper and
middle classes. When eventually working-class people were able
to decide their own pattern of life for themselves, they excluded
from that pattern the Church which had originally excluded
them. Such information offered a welcome release to me in that
it pointed me to some of the *real* problems of mission rather
than the artificial problems I had been trying to solve up till then.
Yet one is still made to feel a little disloyal if one voices facts of
this nature in Church circles.

Of course, it is common for human nature to refuse unpalatable facts of any kind. But I wonder at the kind of ministry that
is being pursued by those ministers and laymen who blink at
such facts. Such denial invalidates the very Gospel that they
claim to preach, for it is the Gospel concerning a Man who
claimed that his Spirit would lead men into all truth. I am certain that Jesus was not referring to what we are pleased to call
religious truth. The Spirit of truth was intended to enable men
to face unpleasant and sordid facts as well as the liberating truth
of God's response to those facts in Jesus Christ.

In his book *The Secular Promise*,[3] Father Martin Jarrett-Kerr
has a chapter entitled 'The Artist as Seismograph'. Like the
scientific instrument designed to measure the slightest tremor in
the earth's crust, so the artist is sensitive to the finest shiftings in

[1] F. Boulard, *An Introduction to Religious Sociology*, trans. M. J. Jack-
son, Darton, Longman and Todd, 1960, p. 16.
[2] E. R. Wickham, *Church and People in an Industrial City*, Lutterworth
Press, 1957.
[3] M. Jarrett-Kerr, *The Secular Promise*, SCM Press, 1964.

society, reflecting them in his work long before people in general are aware of what is happening. The minister, too, should be playing such a role, for it is an essentially prophetic one. Sheer *awareness* of what is going on in the world should be one of the hallmarks of a prophetic ministry, as it was of the Old Testament prophets. The basic sin of the Church is still, as it always was, lack of awareness. It is true that the Church in this country is far more alert to the 'winds of change' in the world generally than it used to be. The most radical resolutions on social issues are passed by church assemblies and councils today with hardly a murmur of dissent, while only ten years ago they would have been hotly contested and maybe even rejected. Pioneer ministries like those in East Harlem and Notting Hill have alerted Christians to problems of which up till recently they were not even aware. But the Church has not noticeably outpaced the rest of the population in the movement towards greater sensitivity to reality. Nor have the Churches in this country been as self-critical of their bourgeois isolation and encapsulation within a social structure as have the Churches, say, in the United States of America. It is significant that the most trenchant criticism of the middle-class suburban church has come from America. Perhaps the dangers there are greater and so require more outspoken criticism. But so much of what the critics say of the Church in America is true of the Church in this country, particularly in the suburbs.

Here again, I can speak from personal experience. I was brought up in the suburbs and reared in a suburban church. I have also ministered in the suburbs, and write, therefore, with appreciation of the real qualities as well as manifest defects of the Church in suburbia. It is with the latter that I concern myself here, and particularly with the fact that, on the whole, the suburban church exists by virtue of *not* listening to what is going on in the society in which it is set. This is due to the very nature of suburban society itself. The suburbs of my youth offered a kind of semi-rural existence in which one could cosily forget the industrialized society of which they were a part. On the whole the suburbs exist to cushion people against the realities of life in an industrialized society. Once isolated in the suburbs one is happily insulated against the forces of change which threaten the stability that we all crave in this rapidly changing world. The churches in the suburbs have been successful, relatively speaking, precisely because they have offered a bastion against change rather than a springboard for change. Colin Williams puts it thus:

There is, in this land (USA), a still greater block (against change), the powerful myth of the 'private'—the feeling that our 'real' life is not in those public worlds, but in the private world of the home. This myth lies behind the powerful bourgeois attempts to maintain, in the outer suburbs, the disappearing forms of family and community life. The business and political life of the outer suburbanite is separated from the home; but in this disturbing world of rapid transition, he still wants the feeling that the old-time values of the home abide; and that this abiding 'private world' is the real world—the eternal world to which he can retreat from the exciting but frightening world of rapid social change. In this attempt, bourgeois man has found in the Church his main ally. It has gone with him to his separate residence world. It has assured him that the home is what really matters. And so, ironically, it would appear that it is precisely *because* the local church is *separated* from business and politics and the pressing problems of society in transition, that bourgeois man has found himself 'at home' in it. We therefore have this ironic but tragic fact that, in many instances, the residence parish congregation is popular precisely because it is irrelevant![4]

In this situation, the prophetic, listening ministry is all the more difficult to exercize because the *raison-d'être* of the suburban church in the minds of most of its members is that it

4 Colin W. Williams, *What in the World?* (companion to *Where in the World?*), Epworth Press, 1965, p. 12.

strengthens the insulation against reality which they are seeking. The best theological insights today are being thrown up in situations where it is almost impossible to ignore such reality even if this were desired, namely in central-city and industrial areas. It is no coincidence that the exciting thinking associated with the writings of John Robinson stems from the highly secularized area of Woolwich. I have already mentioned East Harlem and Notting Hill. I can add that I only came alive theologically (and in other ways) after a move to the Stepney area of East London. The Church in such areas can claim no credit for these insights, for without them it would never have survived. As the late Canon Stanley Evans wrote in his little book *The Church in the Back Streets* :

There is a real sense in which the Church in the back streets is fortunate in a way far beyond populated churches in well-to-do suburbs; these latter can live for a long time yet by evading truth—the former must face truth now or perish.[5]

I do not wish to suggest that there is no role for the suburban church—far from it ! My intention is rather the reverse, i.e. to maintain that a prophetic ministry can and must be exercised within the suburban church. It is a tragedy that the functions of the prophet have become associated purely with extra-parochial ministries, particularly industrial mission in its various forms. That these forms of ministry are genuinely prophetic I do not deny. But prophecy need be no monopoly of such 'public' ministries, as I prefer to call them, when the local residential congregation is prepared to listen to what they have to say about *their* role in the Church's mission. I would define that role in terms of what the local suburban congregation is best equipped to do, and could be better equipped to do, i.e. work with the family and the home. This will always remain one of the chief functions of the local church; in fact, the future of such a church depends upon it

[5] Stanley Evans, *The Church in the Back Streets*, Mowbray, 1962, p. 16.

specializing in this role. The error inherent in the tendency to regard the local parish ministry as the *norm* of all ministry is that it fails to recognize the necessary limitations of its ministry. In the Middle Ages the parish church impinged upon the community at every point. It stood literally at the cross-roads of life. This is not so today. The local church is irrelevant to the needs of all but the most static members of the population, namely children and old people. *But the needs of the others still have to be met.* That is why I plead in the next chapter for more professional expertise in dealing with the problems of emotional and mental adjustment which are the local church's proper concern. But the minister in such a situation can only be a true prophet, and can only lead his congregation in a prophetic ministry, if he listens to the deeper questions raised by the very problems of family-care which he is trying to tackle. These deeper questions concern the nature of the society which is creating the problems of individual and domestic distress which the parish church is attempting to solve. To put it into theological terms they concern the influence of the 'principalities and powers', about which the New Testament, and particularly St Paul, have so much to say.

One of the prime functions of the prophet in the Old Testament was to watch carefully for signs of the influence of suprapersonal powers upon the life of the nation. The prophets painted their warnings upon a broad canvas of world events and structures. They never underestimated the might of the cosmic powers of evil with which man was contending. In recent decades Biblical theologians have taken more and more seriously just what the Bible has to say about the 'principalities and powers'. Far from being primitive concepts, they provide a key for the recognition and interpretation of what Albert H. van den Heuvel calls the 'domination structures' in society today, particularly the political, economic and racial structures which unconsciously shape the lives of all of us. Any ministry claiming to be prophetic must take these cosmic forces seriously into account, and will be forced to do so, once the right questions are asked about the personal problems of the individual which present themselves in the course of the pastoral ministry.

Of course, this prophetic ministry is essentially that of the whole Church, not of the ordained minister only. His task is not to prophesy vicariously on behalf of the Church but to focus and give purpose and direction to the whole Church's prophetic ministry. Any specialist activity in which the minister engages must serve this basic responsibility of discerning the principalities and powers which debar men from their true humanity as summed up in Christ. The minister, therefore, is not required to be a psychotherapist *per se*, or a marriage guidance counsellor, *per se*. In the course of his ministry he may be either of these and many more things besides. But such skills must be a prophetic sign of God's rule over men and God's intention for men. If a minister takes part in any of these activities, it must be in order, partly, to sensitize him to the real questions of human existence to which God addressed himself in Jesus Christ. Only if the minister is directly involved in the muddle and mess of society as a whole will he be able to ensure the fulfilment of the prophetic functions of the whole Church. Without this strict awareness of the prophetic ends which his ministry is serving, the minister will simply become absorbed into unrelated attention to symptoms at the expense of dealing with the real causes of the distortion of man's true humanity.

We are now coming nearer to a more precise definition of the prophetic function of the minister. I have referred to his 'listening' role in society. This listening role is, in fact, part of what might be termed his 'interpretative' role as 'discerning the signs of the times' (Matt. 16.3). The minister is required to interpret both the times in which he lives and the signs of God's activity in those times. This is all part and parcel of his vocation to awareness of what is going on in the world. Of course, the minister will not be consciously *using* pastoral situations for some ulterior motive, however noble and theologically respectable it may be. It would invalidate his pastoral role if he simply betrayed interest in people's problems merely in order to keep himself awake to what is going on in the world. The claims of love must be met unconditionally, as we shall see in the next chapter. But that which makes him a prophet is his ability to interpret to the Church and to the world what in God's name is happening to it (and I mean that literally!). Such an interpretative role no more makes the individual sufferer a means to an end than the teaching activity of a professor of surgery makes his patient on the operating table merely a means of furthering medical research.

In order to interpret what is going on in the world the minister must at some point be making direct contact with the world at its most 'secular'. It is often argued that the minister makes this contact when mixing with the members of his congregation who are, after all, totally immersed in the day-to-day business of industry, commerce and the professions. It may well be that the minister, prior to ordination, served in one of these spheres as what we loosely call a 'layman'. This sounds well in theory but works out badly in practice. It is my experience that ministers on the whole are very little aware of the impact that their church members are making as *lay men and women* upon society. Ministers' evaluation of church members tends to be less in terms of their daily work and more in terms of their status as ecclesiastical animals ('good communicants', 'lukewarm', 'lapsed'!). Church study groups, however well-intentioned, tend to concentrate on 'the Faith', or 'the Church', in other words, with the answers, before exploring in depth the questions posed by the demands of the members' daily occupations.

But there is an even deeper reason why the minister cannot be content to mix only with church members if he is to feel in himself the tensions of secular life. Earlier in this chapter I

pointed out the tendency of church people, particularly in suburban congregations, to want to put daily work and its sordid
concerns behind them when they come to church. Even if they
wish to remain alive to the relevance of the other six days a
week to Sunday, the very pressure to conform to the prevailing
ethos of the 'residential enclave' whose symbol is the suburban
church, is usually too great to maintain this concern; hence the
frustration of so many alert and thinking young lay men and
women in the suburban church. In this situation, it is up to the
minister himself to point the Church to its own secular witness
by personally identifying himself with some secular activity. As
Bill Gowland of the Luton Industrial Mission often says with
reference to industrial chaplaincy : it is good for the minister to
spend at least half a day a week on the shop floor !

Many critics of industrial chaplaincy, full-time or part-time,
state, justly, that however imaginative and sensitive to the
secular situation such a minister may be, he can never identify
himself with it as a layman can. He will always remain a
creature from another world, able to opt out of it at a moment's
notice. We must accept the force of this argument when evalu-
ating the worth-whileness of a minister 'going into the factory'.
It *is* possible for a minister to do industrial chaplaincy and still
remain as clerical in his attitudes as he was before—it is possible,
but not likely. To persist in a difficult and discouraging sphere
such as industry is to have one's illusions about the Church
quickly stripped away. In this situation, any zeal to convert the
ungodly that may have misguidedly animated the minister in
the first place is quickly transformed into zeal to convert the
Church from its ghetto-like mentality into awareness of what is
going on in the world. This, I believe, is why so many ministers
are leaving the parochial ministry for secular work. They may
rationalize their departure in terms of wanting to identify
themselves more closely with the world and its pressures. The
greater motive power is provided, however, by revulsion against

the introversion and self-preoccupation of the typical local church. Any minister who chooses to remain in the parochial ministry and pursue some act of personal involvement, however tenuous, with a secular structure like industry, is going to be nearly torn apart by the tension between two apparent irreconcilables : the claims of mission and the claims of the ecclesiastical institution. It is no wonder that for many ministers the tension becomes insupportable. They either leave the ordained ministry or they surrender to the narcissism of the institution.

The way of prophecy demands, I believe, that the minister accepts the bi-polarity of his role. He will be required to listen to the world by means of some direct encounter with it in order to interpret *to the Church* what is going on, 'whether they will hear or whether they will forbear' (Ezek. 2.5). This will involve him in conflict with both the world and the Church. The pain this causes will be akin to a crucifixion, and the simile is apt in so far as Jesus of Nazareth faced precisely the same problem : alienation from the world ('crucify him, crucify him!') and from his own followers ('they all forsook him and fled!'). I see no way of resolving the tension. It can only be accepted, lived with, and eventually borne in the light of the Man who took this tension upon himself and turned it to victory on the Cross. I speak very personally and humbly here, for I, like so many of my colleagues, have been assailed as much by the hostility of the Church as by that of the world. I do not know which is easier to bear. Either way it creates a situation of conflict *within the minister*, corresponding to the two-way tendency of the personality both to go out and brave the world and to flee from the world into preoccupation with itself. There is a good precedent for this conflict in the prophet Jeremiah :

I did not sit in the company of merrymakers, nor did I rejoice; I sat alone, because thy hand was upon me, for thou hast filled me with indignation. Why is my pain unceasing, my wound incurable, refusing to be healed? Wilt thou be to me like a deceitful brook, like waters that fail?

Therefore thus says the Lord : 'If you return, I will restore you, and you shall stand before me. If you utter what is precious, and not what is worthless, you shall be as my mouth' (Jer. 15.17-19).

So far I have spoken of the listening and interpretative role of the minister simply in terms of listening to the *world*, as if that stood in antithesis to his role of listening to the voice of *God*. There is no antithesis here, for it is from the world that God speaks to the Church. Here is the ultimate warrant for the prophet in his capacity as listener to the world. As recent theologians have been reminding us, it is by penetration into the depths of secular existence that one meets God as the 'Ground of Being', to use Paul Tillich's phrase. We shall explore this thesis more fully in the chapter on the minister as theologian. For the present I would point out one implication of this thought of God as speaking to the Church from the world. The implication is that the Gospel is being just as faithfully, if not more faithfully, preached today by the secular agencies as by the Church.

This conviction was reinforced for me as a result of reading Paul Halmos's book *The Faith of the Counsellors*.[6] This book is a study of the aims and attitudes of members of all the various counselling professions which are growing so much in scope today. These range from psychoanalysts and psychotherapists at one end of the scale to social case-workers of all kinds at the other. In his researches Professor Halmos uncovered a deep discrepancy between what these counsellors consciously avowed as their aims and what they unconsciously exhibited as the real dynamic of their work. Consciously many of them rejected any notion of exercising anything but strictly scientific skills. Unconsciously, however, they were in fact actuated by personal

[6] Paul Halmos, *The Faith of the Counsellors*, Constable, 1965.

concern and even love, though shy of acknowledging these motives. This love exhibited itself in the way members of the counselling professions persisted in their efforts on behalf of their clients, declaring time and again for hope when everything seemed to be hopeless. Underlying everything they did there appeared to be a faith issuing in something very akin to that disinterested love of the other which the New Testament calls *agapē*.

My own acquaintance with social workers of all kinds confirms this view of the Gospel as being preached unconsciously by their expression in professional terms of the principle of suffering love in action. This should surprise nobody who has a sufficiently broad view of God's activity in the world. But it is still common for church people to run down the skills of workers in these fields as 'no substitute for the Gospel'. The only possible Christian response to the evident effectiveness of these skills is (*a*) to rejoice in the sign they present of the Kingdom of God actually coming (Luke 11.20); (*b*) to note Jesus' response to the disciples' attempt to forbid a man to cast out demons in his name 'because he was not following us': 'Do not forbid him; for no one who does a mighty work in my name will be able soon after to speak evil of me. For he that is not against us is for us' (Mark 9.38-40); (*c*) to scrutinize the Church's attempts to preach the Gospel and ask whether they betray the same Christ-like features as are manifest in the attitude of members of the secular 'helping professions' to their clients.

Again, it is part of the prophetic role of the minister, as it is of the whole Church, to interpret what is going on in the world and to discern signs of the Gospel being declared in deed if not in word. Such a vision of the unrestricted activity of God is thoroughly Biblical. It is the lack of such vision which prevents many Christians from allying themselves with secular organizations for fear that they might become tainted with the wrong kind of 'ism'—humanism, communism or whatever other baleful 'ism' one can think of.

Of course, if a minister is to demonstrate this kind of commitment to discernment of the signs of the times, he must have more than a slight degree of detachment both from the world and the Church. Healthy identification with any person or situation can only be achieved by frank recognition of the boundaries between oneself and the person or situation one is seeking to understand. Otherwise one runs the danger of not seeing the wood for the trees. Here I return at the close of this chapter to the problem that faces any minister who seeks to lead the Church in fulfilment of its prophetic role. He is required to be detached from his own congregation and their attempts to make him merely a sounding board for their own fantasies. In the last chapter I dealt more fully with the relationship of minister and congregation and do not wish to repeat myself here. I would only refer to one aspect of this relationship as it affects the prophetic task of the minister.

It is a besetting temptation for a congregation to try to make the minister in their own image. This point is so obvious that it hardly needs elaborating. Ministers know what is meant by the description of a sermon as 'acceptable'. The adjective describes a sermon that is not only appropriate for the occasion but reflects the prejudices and preconceptions of the congregation. It is a fact of human nature that people accept in preaching only what they consciously or unconsciously subscribe to already. The more a minister reflects the prevailing 'ethos' of a congregation the more 'acceptable' he himself tends to be. This fact is bound up with the phenomenon I referred to above of the suburban church as itself a symbol of the bourgeois aspirations of the suburban community. Within the Church itself the minister, particularly in the Presbyterian tradition, tends in his turn to become the symbol of the congregation's own ideals of respectability and acceptability. This is a far cry from the Presbyterian insistence on the place of prophecy in the Church, but I am beginning seriously to doubt whether the much-vaunted Presbyterian feeling for the prophetic is not something of a myth. In practice, if not in theory, Presbyterian congregations are as little interested in prophecy as those of any other denomination.

This picture of the minister as subservient to the bourgeois ideals projected upon him by the congregation would appear to contradict what I said in the last chapter about the clerical domination of the Church. Surely, it may be argued, one cannot have it both ways. If the clergy are the lynch-pin of the Church, then they could hardly be accused of subservience to their congregations. The dependence of the flock upon the minister, however infantile, should, it would seem, offer some opportunity for the minister to give a prophetic lead to his people. The argument is attractive but false. For we are not dealing here with a situation of one-way dependence, i.e. of congregation upon the minister. We are dealing here with a situation of mutual (and infantile) dependence of minister and people upon each other. The desire of the latter to put the minister on a pedestal is matched by his equally strong desire to be put on a pedestal. Ministers, more than most, need to play the role assigned to them by the Church because often enough they are deep down unaware of their own personal identity.

As long as no real attempt is made to help ministers-in-training to insight into the possibility of their own neurotic collusion with the dependency needs of the congregation, we shall continue to have a ministry insufficiently detached in a healthy fashion for the prophetic role which is its sole *raison d'être*. Once ministers are given sufficient inward freedom to be real persons instead of the puppets they often are, the stage will be set for the growth of a Church which is faithful to the future instead of being merely enslaved by the past. Such a Church may lose a great many of its members in the process, for it will no longer be the bulwark against change that they expect the

Church to be. On the other hand, such a Church will be a more secure bastion of faith in so far as it will direct people more effectively to their sole and ultimate security in Christ 'the same yesterday, today and forever'. To know such a security is to be set free for that commitment to the unknown future which is the essence of the Christian faith.

4

The Listener

T H E essential ingredient of any effective pastorate must be the ability to listen. The importance of this cannot be taken too seriously. For so much mental distress is caused by the failure of people to command the wholehearted attention of the significant persons in their lives. In the very first few years of life the child receives his sense of personal identity from the seriousness with which he is listened to by his parents. In their ability to respond to his needs, at an age when he can do little to justify his existence in their eyes, lies the key to the growth of a sense of personal dignity and worth. It is generally accepted today by workers in all the 'helping professions' that emotional and personality disorders derive from a breakdown of inter-personal relationships within the original family setting. A child who has never, or only rarely, been 'listened to' with any seriousness by his parents will himself become withdrawn and self-preoccupied to the extent of being unable, in his turn, to bestow self-forgetful attention upon others, including any children that he may eventually have. So the problem is handed down from generation to generation. In extreme cases, the resulting damage to personality is so great as to require the description, and the treatment appropriate to, 'schizophrenia'. On a lesser scale, the problem presents itself in an inability to trust, to identify with and, ultimately, to love other people. If communication is to be in any measure restored for such sufferers, then the minister must first supply the ingredient lacking in the original impaired relationship, namely, his loving attention and his utter willingness to listen before ever he opens his mouth.

We can all testify on the very simplest level to the healing power of listening. How often we have despaired of helping a parishioner, so intractable does his problem appear to be, only to be surprised at the relief which the simple act of listening to his problem has brought to him. 'A burden shared is a burden halved' is no trite formula. But before a minister can listen effectively he must be aware of the importance of the listening process. By the quality of his listening the pastor can lead a parishioner to levels of insight quite inaccessible by any other means. Such listening creates the setting in which the sufferer can begin to listen to himself and view his own problems in a fresh perspective. To achieve this result the pastor must be prepared to face the pain of listening to others. This means training him to recognize and interpret his own automatic reactions to what the other person is saying. There is still, however, a great deal of resistance amongst ministers and in theological colleges to the idea of such training. This is, as I have already pointed out, in marked contrast to the sphere of social work, where casework training based upon psycho-analytical principles is rapidly becoming the rule. It would, of course, be unfair not to acknowledge the growing acceptance of the need for psychological training for the pastoral ministry evident in the interest aroused, in England, by conferences of the 'Institute of Religion and Medicine' and the courses arranged by 'Christian Teamwork', the 'Guild of Pastoral Psychology' and the 'Clinical Theology Association'. But such courses are usually made available to ministers who have been in the pastoral ministry for a few years at least. I can see the point of the argument that the experienced minister will gain more benefit from the courses than a theological student. But this is more a criticism of theological training for not giving the ordinand enough opportunity

for work in the parish setting to allow the course of psychological training to make sense. I have heard it argued that if
theological students were given such training they would be
tempted to leave the ministry from the very start. I can well
understand the sentiment, for I too felt strongly moved to leave
the ministry under the impact of such training received later in
my ministry. Again, however, the onus of responsibility for this
situation must rest upon the Church which makes it so manifestly difficult for ministers to apply their psychological insights
to the pastoral situation, and which itself comes under judgment
once the true nature of the traditional relationship between
minister and congregation is perceived.

Something of this resistance to psychological insights is
apparent in the otherwise excellent British Council of Churches
document *The Shape of the Ministry*, to which I referred above.
In the section on theological training headed 'other studies' the
report calls for 'some training in pastoral psychology; this should
be sufficient at any rate for day-to-day requirements and to
enable the presbyter to recognize conditions which need more
professional psychiatric assistance. An introduction to psychiatric work along the lines of the course being developed at Selly
Oak ought to be considered, so long as it was understood by the
men concerned that this was an introduction only, *and did not
qualify them to act as amateur practitioners.*'[1]

The nervousness with which the working party treat the field
of pastoral psychology is evident in the last sentence. What else
is the minister to be if not a 'practitioner' in human relationships? The word 'amateur' is pejorative and unhelpful in this
context. If it is used to stress the dangers of ministers attempting
to tackle psychological problems beyond their competence, then
the word might be justified. But the greater danger resides in
ministers attempting, as they do at the moment, to tackle the
normal pastoral problems of their ministry without being able to

[1] *The Shape of the Ministry*, p. 58.

recognize and deal with the neurotic component in most, if not all, such problems. Candidates for the field of social casework are expected to be able to treat as well as recognize the minor forms of neurosis, and are often, in fact, trained to do so by professional psychoanalysts. Such treatment is mediated by the listening, caring relationship which is the theme of this chapter. Such listening and caring require a degree of insight in the minister which can only be gained from a training in which pastoral psychology has a higher place than that so timidly conceded by the writers of the B.C.C. Report.

The fact of course is that 'psychology' is a loaded word. In my experience, reference to the workings of human personality always arouses varying degrees of anxiety and apprehension in the listener. Ministers with more rigid and defended personalities tend to react strongly against attempts to mediate insight, which they construe as a form of attack upon them. No one can be blamed for this situation, which is created by unconscious factors within the personality. One may well ask, however, whether such compulsive resistance to insight is not a disqualification for the pastoral ministry. The basis for insight into other people's problems can only be provided by insight into one's own. So much havoc is wrought in the Church by the situation of mutual projection between minister and congregation getting out of hand that the importance of psychological training cannot be over-emphasized. I do not say this lightly, for no one is more aware than I of the pain and veritable 'harrowing of hell' that accompany such growth into insight. Perhaps it is not required of every minister that he should specialize in acquiring psychological skills, but he should be imbued with sufficient to enable him to deal with the normal healthy personality at points of minor breakdown.

This statement requires underlining. The best use to which a minister's psychological training can be put is in helping with the normal problems of normal people. The greatest service

Freud did was to provide a basis for insight into the workings of the normal person's mind. To use a crude analogy: just as the sport of motor-racing provides the manufacturer with data that can be used for the manufacture of the ordinary family saloon, so the researches of the clinical psychologist can help to refine and render more effective the minister's work with people facing quite routine problems. The minister who follows a course in pastoral psychology may never need to take up counselling in depth. He will have been immeasurably strengthened, however, for his main task: that of listening constantly for the real questions that people are asking him.

The most valuable preparation for a listening ministry is that which enables a minister to listen to himself and his own reactions to what people are saying to him. It is impossible for even the most skilled listener to be unaffected inwardly by the emotional overtones of the speaker's words. Sympathetic vibrations are bound to be set up in him by the emotional content of what is uttered. It is the listener's ability to *interpret* to himself his own reactions to the speaker that turns the phenomenon of 'collusion' into a means of insight into the speaker's condition. In other words, what I feel about the parishioner, rightly interpreted, yields valuable evidence of the state of his feelings towards me.

It is axiomatic in all social casework training today that the worker should be guided to ask of any personal relationship in which he is professionally engaged: What is the other person doing to me? The ability to ask this question and answer it fruitfully helps to create that combination of involvement and detachment which is required in any professional listener. The psychological term used to describe this kind of involvement in the other person's state of mind is 'empathy'. 'Empathy' is more than 'sympathy' (suffering with . . .). Its strict meaning is 'suffering in . . .', and implies the ability to put oneself in the other person's shoes and actually feel what he is feeling. The detachment which is a corollary of empathy enables the listener to interpret these feelings in a way helpful to the speaker. This faculty of interpreting one's own subjective reactions to the parishioner is not acquired easily. It is true that some ministers possess a natural gift for empathy with others, according to the measure of imagination, sympathy and insight with which nature has endowed them. But even such gifted persons would not fail to profit from the training in the art of listening which is the essence of any worth-while course in pastoral psychology. The basic justification for such training is simple : listening always arouses anxiety in the listener. The extent to which he is made the object of both negative and positive transference is the extent to which his repressed anxieties and feelings of insecurity and guilt are liable to be evoked by the same anxieties and feelings in the parishioner. A minister who can cope with the painful aspects of the listening relationship is thereby released from himself in such a way as to be genuinely free to listen to what the other person is saying.

I said earlier on that the minister is not required merely to recognize emotional distress when he sees it, but actually to treat it where appropriate. There are several reasons why this responsibility must be assumed by the minister, the first being the simple fact that, whether he likes it or not, people still choose to come to him and only to him with their personal problems.

Some of these problems arise naturally out of the normal demands made upon the clerical profession. I have found that the 'occasional offices' often provide a 'way in' to the deeper problems agitating the minds of those who request them, particularly the sacrament of baptism. Young parents often have genuine anxieties about their capacity to rear a new-born child. My own technique of baptismal preparation is to begin, not with any doctrinal statements about the sacrament but with a simple explanation of the significance for the child of his earliest relationships with mother and father. This can, and often does, lead on to a frank disclosure of some of the normal but none-theless bothersome problems of love-hate feelings towards the child, brother-sister jealousy of the new baby, and the changes in the husband-wife relationship caused by the advent of a child. From this point it is but a short step to meaningful explanation of the sacrament in terms of God's total acceptance of us in Jesus Christ, declared and sealed in his life, death and resurrection. Such an approach to baptismal preparation is far more helpful than the defensive tactics of 'fencing the sacrament' against parents who have little conception of what it means. If the sacrament of baptism declares God's unconditional acceptance of his children in Jesus Christ, then that meaning will best be mediated by a minister who starts with the parents where they are and leads them on through discussion of real questions to the central Christian affirmations enshrined in the sacrament.

Marriage preparation provides a similar basis for mediating insight into the deeper personal problems. Young couples pre-paring for marriage are very open to the ministrations of a pastor who is able to sense the hidden anxieties and fears which assail them when poised on the brink of marriage. A simple explanation of two of the basic anxieties in marriage—commit-ment anxiety and separation anxiety—can help to prepare young marrieds for the inevitable ebb and flow of feeling within mar-riage. Commitment anxiety is aroused at the point of the couple's deep involvement with and exposure to each other. Such close involvement can evoke memories of the hurt caused to a child in infancy by his trust in mother being violated as a result of her inability to give him the loving attention he required. He tries to avoid further hurt by withdrawing into preoccupation with himself and a compulsive refusal to commit himself to any deep personal relationship. It is easy to see how the commitment to a partner in marriage will arouse, through the transference situa-tion, the same anxiety as was experienced in infancy. It is not

c

uncommon for newly-weds to spring apart emotionally once they realize the binding nature of their commitment. At the same time such flight from each other generally arouses the opposite anxiety, namely separation anxiety. This anxiety concerns the threat of isolation and possibly death posed for the infant by his failure to get mother's attention. The panic caused by separation from the beloved object creates a situation of 'hysterical' flight towards her and leads to attempts to force her to take notice of him. Again it is easy to see how the same anxiety can be aroused in marriage. The mechanism of flight from each other, activated by commitment anxiety, leads to the counter-reaction of flight towards each other activated by separation anxiety. A trained pastor can help prepare a young couple for these swings of feeling, in order that they should not become too alarmed by them. Such marriage preparation, based on deep insight into basic trends in human nature, will 'speak to' the condition of the couple concerned in a way that formal instruction in the Christian teaching on marriage cannot. At the same time, the Christian teaching will appear more meaningful when it is based upon a couple's heightened awareness of the workings of the marriage relationship. A special responsibility for communicating such awareness rests upon the minister who undertakes to remarry a partner in a divorce case. This is not the place to argue the rights and wrongs of remarriage in church. But if a minister accepts the responsibility for solemnizing such marriages he must also accept responsibility for examining with the partner concerned the deeper factors leading to failure in the first marriage. The readiness to make such an examination is generally all the greater when the minister is seen to disregard the legal categories of 'guilt' or 'innocence' and treats the situation as one of mutual breakdown in the marital relationship. In this way the foundation can be laid for a more stable and happy second marriage.

The other 'occasional office' required of the minister is the funeral. Here again the minister can assist the bereaved far more effectively if he is able to recognize and treat the neurotic component that is present in any bereavement. Mourning is often accompanied by a great deal of neurotic guilt over the failure of the mourners to value and support the deceased in the way they feel they ought to have done. The death of a loved member of the family can be rendered more painful by the repressed memory of infantile death-wishes directed towards that member of the family, particularly a parent, by his dependents. The death by natural causes of, say, a mother can seem to represent the fulfilment of the murderous thoughts that she is bound to have aroused occasionally in her children. In such cases, the minister needs to recognize the refusal to be comforted as the expression of guilt unacknowledged and therefore incapable, as it stands, of forgiveness. In this situation the minister's counselling skills can be tactfully and sensitively deployed in the treatment of a neurotic condition. Not all bereavements will require this depth of pastoral care, but readiness to deal with the more serious situations cannot fail to help the minister in coping with the more normal and less emotionally harrowing bereavements.

The three supreme crises of birth, marriage and death are the points at which a minister's professional pastoral skills are most obviously required. But neurotic situations requiring treatment come in other guises as well. Before the minister can decide whether to refer a parishioner to a more specialized agency for help he must be able to recognize and make a minimum diagnosis of the situation. This is especially so where he is confronted by a 'psychosis' (insanity). But a minister's training must be such that he will not be panicked into rejecting a parishioner merely because his problem requires specialist treatment. Ignorance of psychological facts can only encourage the premature rejection of a sufferer by a minister whose own anxieties have got out of hand. The first question a minister must ask is: Why did this person choose to come to me in the first place? A minister's pastoral responsibility towards a parishioner needing referral can only be discharged if he continues to offer him loving support during the course of his specialist treatment. For the fact remains that it was he who was first selected as confidant by the sufferer. To that extent the minister has had a claim laid upon him which he dare not ignore or reject by too abrupt a referral to another agency.

Here we must again remind ourselves of the basic pastoral task, which is that of listening and opening up channels of communication which have become blocked or were, perhaps, never opened. Any pastoral contact, however trivial, may prove to be the point of departure for helping a sufferer in depth. In the first instance, the parishioner may present the basic problem in the guise of some lesser and more trivial problem. The church attender who has unaccountably given up church-going may, in fact, be appealing for pastoral care. This phenomenon is in line with what is known today about the different levels at which people communicate their deepest needs and longings. Rarely are these needs and longings verbalized; in fact, it is the inability to verbalize them that creates the problem in the first place. The ability to verbalize one's feelings depends upon the establishment of trust between speaker and listener. It also depends upon lowering the level of censorship in a personal relationship to the point where the speaker can express what he really feels without fear of rejection by the listener. For it is precisely this fear of rejection which ensures the persistence of neurotic guilt within the personality long after the original guilt-provoking situation has passed into oblivion.

A major task in pastoral work is the handling of neurotic guilt. Unfortunately the clergy are often tempted to trade upon feelings of neurotic guilt in the parishioner. This temptation can only be avoided by insight on the part of the minister into the nature of his own guilt feelings and awareness of the tendency to project these feelings upon the congregation. The power of these guilt feelings derives from the compulsive need to hide the truth about our aggressive feelings from ourselves and others. Behind the whole phenomenon of neurotic guilt lies the basic fear of rejection by others if aggressive feelings are allowed to erupt upon them. This is where the minister, as the parent-figure in the congregation, can help a great deal by understanding and demonstrating his awareness of people's need to express and come to terms with their feelings of aggression. As a minister he will inevitably be the focus of aggressive and hostile feelings. At the same time he will represent the very punishment that his parishioners feel they deserve because of their aggressive feelings. The sight of the dog-collar tends to evoke guilt feelings in others; hence, possibly, the truth of the fact that if a parson wishes to have a compartment to himself in a train, he only needs to wear his dog-collar !

The minister's ability to cope with the problem of aggression in others depends upon his ability to accept his own aggression and the guilt it provokes. Only so will the sight of aggression in others not stimulate him to the censoriousness which is as much a condemnation of his own aggression as theirs. As depression arising from the repression of strong feelings of hostility is one of the commonest pastoral problems, I will concentrate upon the counselling of parishioners suffering from this form of neurosis. This is not, of course, a case-history but a brief sketch of a pastoral-counselling situation compressed almost to the point of caricature.

A discerning minister will be aware of fluctuations of mood and feeling in members of his congregation. He will also have been approached from time to time by people who are feeling more than just the 'one degree under' of the 'Aspro' advertisements. Life seems to have become one round of weariness to the parishioner (whom I shall refer to in this context as 'the client'). He can hardly drag himself out of bed in the morning. He is constantly tired, although he may feel a little brighter at the end of the day. He has become difficult to live with and he cannot stand the company of others. Such a change of mood in a man previously able to cope may be coupled, so the minister discovers on enquiry, with a change of circumstances at work, e.g. the arrival of a new and difficult boss. The client can do nothing but bemoan his lot as a complete and utter failure. Here already the trained minister will detect the outlines of a 'reactive depression' ('reactive' because it arises as a reaction to circumstances prevailing at the time). The depression stems from the client's unconscious attempt to repress the anger provoked by his frustrating boss-figure. The anger is not *created* by the boss's behaviour, but only *triggered off* by it; it is a repressed anger stemming from the earliest frustrations experienced in infancy. The minister will gradually compile a case history of the client out of the pastoral dialogue with him. This case history will not be elicited by formal question and answer but will be compiled from information presented by the client in his own way and at his own pace. The very facts that the client selects for presentation and the significant omission of other facts will tell the pastor a great deal about the areas of greatest mental pain affecting the client. The case history will include information about the client's current complaint, its onset and previous occasions of it, his family history, his previous personal history (childhood, school, work, adolescence, marital history, etc.), his previous personality (i.e. what kind of person was he before the trouble began?) and his religious attitudes. The period of recording the case history may extend over several interviews or be completed at the very first meeting. After the necessary data have been elicited the pastor must make a diagnosis, which will take account of the relationship between the personality pattern of the client (conditioned as it was by early experiences in infancy and the subsequent course of his life history) and the effect upon him of contemporary events. This diagnosis will take account not merely of the facts of the client's suffering but of its causes.

The pastor will not be over-hasty in interpreting these causes to the client, for, if unprepared for them, he will either reject them or be raised to a level of anxiety inhibitive of insight. Only as the client can begin to trust the pastor as a man will he gradually venture to acknowledge to himself the real state of his feelings and begin to express them. In the case of depression there will be a certain amount of 'testing out' of the pastor by the client. The safer the client feels with the pastor the more he will tend to transfer to him the repressed feelings of anger aroused by the original parent-child relationship. It is the pastor's acceptance of this hostility without rejecting the client which is the healing element in the pastoral dialogue. For the first time in his life, maybe, the client can acknowledge his anger towards mother and father, figures whom he previously idealized in order to hide the deep-seated anger they aroused in him.

In the course of such pastoral counselling the pressure of neurotic guilt will gradually be lifted and for the first time the client will be able to accept responsibility for genuinely guilty behaviour without falling prey to the exaggerated self-condemnation attaching to even the most trivial peccadillo. At this point the pastor can begin to mediate forgiveness to the client, for he is now in a position to forgive himself. Also at this point the pastor can begin to speak in explicit terms of the Gospel and its record of a Man who took the full force of men's hatred upon himself at Calvary and still declared his persecutors accepted and forgiven to all eternity. The accepting relationship of pastor and client is but a pale reflection of God's total acceptance of men in Jesus Christ. But only as the client begins to feel in his bones what it means to be accepted as he is by another human being will he have any clue about what the Gospel is really saying. This cannot be urged too strongly. Ministers are too easily prone to making metaphysical assertions in a vacuum. This is particularly true of preaching, as we shall see, but it applies also to religious statements made in the course of individual pastoral work. The ability of a parishioner to accept and understand the content of a 'faith statement' depends to a large extent upon his personal experience of seeing the reality of those statements embodied in his relationship with the counsellor. The fear is often expressed that pastoral counselling, by disclosing the effect of past experiences upon present behaviour, weakens the sense of responsibility in the sufferer. In fact, the opposite is the case. The clearing of neurotic guilt always paves the way for acknowledgment of genuinely guilty conduct. Such acknowledgment opens the door to the reception of forgiveness and real 'amendment of life'. Far from psychological insight making people *less* responsible it makes them *more* responsible. Freedom from one's unconscious and compulsive needs means freedom to act responsibly towards others. Such freedom is never complete, of course, for growth to maturity is a slow process. But the forces of healing and wholeness within the psyche, once activated, continue to work insidiously, breaking down resistances, knitting together the split and torn ego and bestowing that inner unity, and thus humanity, of which the Man of Nazareth is the full and final norm.

Not all emotional problems are susceptible to treatment in an individual counselling relationship. In my experience, limited though it is, the face-to-face relationship of pastor and client most helps people with depressive and schizoid personality problems. The hysterical, attention-seeking person and the paranoid person with strong persecutory feelings are more easily helped, if at all, in a group setting. House groups provide a possible context for that 'sharing in depth' which is a prerequisite for insight into one's own needs. Much psychotherapeutic work is based these days upon the group. I can only mention briefly my own tentative experience in this field. In my Stepney congregation, we had two house groups meeting once a month. One of the groups consisted half of churchgoers and half of non-churchgoers. The depth of sharing obtained in the group made the distinction irrelevant. My aim with this group was to make it a place where people could talk freely and frankly about their basic anxieties, hopes and longings. We tried, in other words, to be a genuinely therapeutic group. With some of the members there was a marked growth of stability and poise as a result. The leader of such a group must have some training in the principles of group dynamics if he is to cope with the varying levels of anxiety that such a group produces. But it is the basic contention of this book that such training should be a must for every minister. The second group consisted mainly of women, several of them also non-churchgoers. This was a more specialized group in that it mainly discussed problems of family and the home. This again proved a valuable lead-in to the frank airing of personal difficulties and the possibility of enhanced insight for members of the group.

Any minister who embarks on pastoral counselling will quickly realize the need for a Church which is a genuinely accepting, therapeutic community. It is not within the scope of this book to discuss the precise way in which the congregation can become such a community. But the reader will not fail to notice that the questions I have asked about the prophetic and pastoral role of the minister raise even larger questions about the nature of the Church's response to the needs of those 'who are as sheep without a shepherd'. Any acceptance by ministers of the insights derived from the other helping professions will entail scrutiny of the manifest failure of the Church to be the healing and saving community it is intended to be. It is perhaps the awareness of the vast changes such scrutiny will involve for the institutional life of the Church that creates the hesitation of the Church to commit itself to the implementing of these insights. If such hesitation prevails the Church will indeed deserve the judgment accruing to those of whom Jesus said, sorrowfully : 'You did not know the time of your visitation' (Luke 19.44).

5

The Theologian

THIS book is written against the background of a crisis of status affecting the ordained ministry at the present time. Like the general practitioner in medicine, only more so, the minister no longer enjoys the social prestige that he once had. Much of the flight from the pastoral ministry can be ascribed to this loss of status. Those who remain within this ministry are tempted, understandably, to find compensation in preoccupation with ecclesiastical bureaucracy. But ministers are being driven from even this bastion by the current emphasis upon the greater role of the laity in the government of the Church. It is no wonder that in this situation ministers are heard to ask : 'What is there left for the minister to do?'

My purpose is to provide a very personal but, I hope, realistic answer to that question. I welcome the gradual stripping away of ministerial status and prerogatives as an essential preparation for acceptance of the minister's true task as a prophet. The minister's 'pastoral work' must also have its prophetic basis to be rightly the concern of the minister. To define that prophetic basis and to help the whole Church to fulfil its prophetic function is the task of the minister as *theologian*.

Gibson Winter describes the minister's part in assisting what he terms 'the lay apostolate' thus :

At present, the clergyman is trained as a theological specialist and yet works as a personal counsellor and administrative expert.

This is the contradiction inherent in theological training within our secularized world. Theological schools are torn two ways by this situation, for they wish to make the theological training more relevant, and yet they are convinced that a clergyman should be trained primarily for theological reflection and preaching. In the present structure, this is an insoluble dilemma. If, on the other hand, the laity are the apostolate of the Church, then we need clergy or religious specialists who are theologically prepared to give time and attention to working with laity. This means that preaching, personal care, cultic activity and administrative work would take a very secondary place in the work of the theological specialists. Preaching in the worldly structures, where it occurs, would be a layman's task. The clergyman is primarily needed as a theological resource for this lay apostolate.[1]

When this lay apostolate is taken seriously by the Church there need not, I believe, be any contradiction between (*a*) the need to make theological training more relevant and (*b*) the need to train clergymen for theological reflection and preaching. If a minister is trained under (*a*) in the appropriate skills shared by the minister with the other 'secular' helping professions (the necessity for which training I have been arguing so far), then his need under (*b*) for training as a theologian will be more adequately met. For his theology will then become an *answering* theology and an *interpreting* theology, able both to discern and define the nature of God's saving activity as it is seen in the world. Such a theology will inevitably be more relevant to the training of the laity in their apostolate, in so far as it takes seriously, as its proper sphere of enquiry, the world in which the layman is daily involved, and in which God is seen as present and active.

Again, I must reiterate that theology came alive for me only when I experienced training in the field of psychotherapy. From that moment my theology became the interpretation of this experience in terms of the divine activity I believe it to have

[1] Gibson Winter, *The New Creation as Metropolis*, The Macmillan Co., 1963, pp. 92 ff.

been. This is, of course, simply to state the obvious, namely that the theologian must know personally what he is talking about. Theological concepts can only come alive when viewed in relation to a 'disclosure situation' personal to the theologian concerned. For me, that disclosure situation was provided by a training in pastoral counselling. Not every theologian would be required to submit to this particular discipline in order to have theological truth disclosed to him. But however the truth is mediated the requirement in every case will be the same: an experience of personal liberation, whether mediated by psychological or other means. Without such an experience of liberation on the part of the theologian, it will hardly be possible for him to assist the laity theologically in their apostolate. For they can hardly be expected to profit from a theology which has no roots in a genuine personal experience of the theologian himself.

I am not at all certain, however, that the 'freedom of a Christian man' is very evident in the general life of the Church as I have seen it. The Church claims to hold the key to salvation in terms of release from the fetters of sin, but, as Monica Furlong points out, the facts belie this claim:

The Church has encouraged us to believe that all that is needed for spiritual health is the routine of prayer and the liturgy, of confession and the sacraments. These things are, of course, infinitely precious, a life-giving and sanity-preserving framework and more besides; the foretaste of the abundant living talked about in the Gospels. Yet the disturbing fact remains that too many who faithfully practise these things do not seem liberated people. If one spends much time amongst practising Christians one does find people who have been strangely and marvellously liberated by them and by the loving which springs from them. Yet the disturbing fact remains that too many who faithfully practise these things do not seem liberated people, but people as narrow, or more narrow, than those who have never been exposed to the faith.[2]

[2] M. Furlong, *With Love to the Church*, Hodder and Stoughton, 1965, p. 62.

A living theology must be rooted in a living experience of the liberating power of the Gospel once it has really been allowed to become 'good news' to people within the Church, not least the ministers themselves. For theology is nothing if not reflection upon experience. Yet still the Church concentrates on trying to teach theology without mediating the experience of release into freedom from oneself and freedom for others which is the basis of it. That is why I am suspicious of the current cry for more doctrinal teaching in the Church. There is at the moment a great demand for more 'teaching' about 'the Faith' on the part of lay men and women of all denominations. The demand is being supplied by study courses and outlines of various kinds, neatly packaged into convenient chunks for digestion by house and study groups from one 'season' to another. I am not decrying the importance of such courses or of the 'teaching weeks' and 'teaching sermons' which are current fare in all churches. But even the slightest awareness of the learning process must arouse doubts about the efficacy of such didacticism. In this connection we must heed the warning of Albert H. van den Heuvel in an article on ecumenical education published in the World Council of Churches' Bulletin, *Study Encounter* :

The experience is humiliating. There was that top-notch German theological student. He had gone through all the classes of the big ecumenical scholars; he had read, *à fond*, the reports of Amsterdam, Evanston and New Delhi; he was even one of those rare animals who read the 'Ecumenical Review'. After his studies at home he had, as a matter of course, received a W.C.C. scholarship for study at a theological school of another confession in another land. And then he showed up as a work camper in a Youth Department work camp. It was after those four weeks of building a country road that he wrote to us, 'Now I know what the ecumenical movement is all about !'

He is not alone. Time and time again we hear from people, less qualified and less prepared, but similarly declaring that only by *doing* have they discovered what they were looking for. Involvement is apparently an absolutely necessary, or—if you want to put it negatively—an absolutely inevitable element in education. Preparation, knowledge, information, an idea, can be gained by listening and reading, but education that is really worthy of the term is to be received only through involvement.[3]

The Gospel of liberation cannot be communicated on the verbal level alone. People will only sense what the Gospel is about when they draw the stuff of their theology from relationships with others which are the very embodiment of that Gospel.

Most theological education, however, never gets 'under the skin' of those who are the recipients of it. I found this to be sadly true for myself during that period of my ministry when I was running away from the 'shadow-side' of my nature. Preaching was a painful effort because it did not spring from the depths of my being. I literally had nothing to say. I knew nothing of the God of love about whom I was required to speak; hence the lack of congruity between my conscious profession of the Gospel and my unconscious orientation towards Law. My change of outlook came about when I discovered that the God whom I had been worshipping had been nothing but a projection of infantile fears aroused by the earliest personal relationships I had ever known. He was a God to be placated because such had been the nature of my relationship with my own father. The basic model of my theology was provided by an experience of having to earn status in the eyes of others because of a lack of inner certainty about what that status might be. Such earning of status could only be carried through on the basis of the repression into the unconscious of elements in my personality which might, so I thought, jeopardize the whole operation. It was only in the setting of a therapeutic group that I could begin to acknowledge to myself and to others the facts about my nature which I feared would, if declared and expressed, secure my rejection. The miracle of

[3] Albert H. van den Heuvel, 'We shall know only what we do', *Study Encounter*, World Council of Churches, Vol. 1, No. 4, 1965, p. 189.

finding, in the process, acceptance and forgiveness, laid the foundation for a new theological model which tallied with, rather than contradicted, my unconscious feelings. I was now able to read the Gospel in the light of an experience of its truth for *me*. *I* had been accepted, despite all the most unacceptable elements in my nature. *I* had not been required to justify my existence to others. *I* had been valued as an individual worthy in his own right. *I* had been released into a measure of freedom that I had never before possessed. Psychotherapy had done for me what no amount of preaching and traditional pastoral care had even begun to achieve in my life hitherto.

This does not mean that psychology became a 'substitute for the Gospel', as is often feared. Psychology proved, instead, to be the instrument of the Gospel. It made real for me just what the Gospel was saying and it provided me with a model on which I could base all my reflection on and preaching of the Gospel. The experience on a human level of being accepted *in toto* prior to any ability on my part to justify my existence embodied, however imperfectly, God's total acceptance of the world in Jesus Christ. The sense of personal identity, the nourishment of spirit and the status mediated by membership of an accepting group found their endorsement in the New Testament proclamation of the gift of sonship, by which we can address God intimately as 'Daddy' (Romans 8.15). A new zest for living, a greater physical and emotional buoyancy, and an urge to creative activity, flowed from this enhanced awareness of a status which no longer depended on my efforts to justify my existence. Because I was no longer *required* to achieve anything I felt freer to fulfil the commitments laid upon me. Again, I found endorsement for this experience in the New Testament teaching about the gifts of the Spirit, and, above all, in the narrative of Pentecost.

This interpretation of the Gospel in the light of a personal subjective experience might appear to involve a dangerous narrowing down of the Gospel into merely a panacea for individual

problems of emotional adjustment. Such a view would be alien
to the theology into which I was initiated by this experience. For
my own personal spiritual crisis proved to be only the starting-
point for a theology which took account of the need for the
redemption of the whole of society. Above all, it gave me a
theology which made sense of the Church's mission in a highly
secularized society. Hitherto my notions of evangelism had been
based upon what I discovered to be a fallacy, namely, that
mission had as its aim the making of people into something
they were not already. I have already described my feelings on
first arriving in Stepney. When I first came there I was intimi-
dated by the sight of blocks of flats inhabited by thousands of
people who seemed, somehow, to belong to another camp. 'We'
of the Church stood over against 'them' of the world. This
dichotomy vanished with the awareness that, in fact, we all
belonged to the same camp, as those who had all been declared
accepted by God in Jesus Christ. The only possible difference
between the Church and the world was that we of the Church
were supposed to *know* the fact of man's acceptance by God
whereas those of the world did not. It then became all too
obvious to me that the 'Church' as I knew it needed as much
redeeming as 'the world', in so far as so many churchgoers are
manifestly *not* aware of how they stand with God. The pursuit
of justification by works out of blindness to the lack of necessity
for such pursuit is all too evident in the middle-class Church
of our day. It is also evident in much preaching, as I realized
on scrutinizing the sermons I had written before my own breakthrough into fresh awareness of what the Gospel was saying. Not
that my sermons in the previous era differed greatly in content
from those preached subsequently. But the emphasis shifted
subtly and decisively from the theme, 'You *cannot* justify yourself before God' (logical conclusion: despair), to 'you *need not*
attempt to justify yourself before God' (logical conclusion:
freedom).

Any acceptance of the proper distinction between 'the Church' and 'the world' in terms of the distinction between those who are *aware* of how they stand with God (or rather how God stands with them) and those who are not, has enormous consequences for our view of preaching. Preaching, in the narrower sense of pulpit utterance, will begin to reflect what is the concern of the whole Church in its pastorate to the world, namely God's acceptance of all men as declared in Jesus Christ. Moralism in the pulpit is banished in consequence. The congregation will not be exhorted to do anything at all except reflect upon the facts of their acceptance by God. Preaching which is genuinely a call to reflection upon the fact of God's acceptance of all men must be an important element in any renewal of the Church, for it will embody the prophetic concern for the destruction of the idols who are the real objects of worship in most congregations today. How else can we explain the moralism of so much 'preaching' carried on in pulpits up and down the land? Any sermon which uses those deadly words 'ought', 'try', 'duty', 'if only . . .', etc., with which my own sermons used to be peppered, is a summons to worship of a false god, the god of infantile projections, anxieties and taboos. Such projections are basically idolatrous. Like the primitive idol, they are powerless to conduct the worshipper from narcissistic preoccupation with himself. Nor can they ever provide the basis for a Church which is genuinely a therapeutic community, for, if left uncorrected, they confirm the worshipper in an essentially immature state of mind.

If preaching is to be rescued from the dangers attaching to projection of distorted images of God, the minister must both possess and mediate insight into these projections. Neither of these aims can be achieved easily. I have already referred several times to the pain which must accompany any growth into insight on the part of the minister. Similar pain will be aroused in the minds of the congregation by preaching which 'gets under their skin' precisely because it is conducted in awareness of the basic human anxieties and longings. If preaching is a declaration of God's acceptance of mankind in Jesus Christ, then it must involve the evoking of the very feelings which members of the congregation are repressing lest the acknowledgment of them—to themselves, to others and to God—should bring about the feared rejection. In other words, preaching must help to bring to awareness the unacceptable feelings in the minds of the congregation in order that they can then be declared accepted. Such preaching in depth is far from merely 'psychological preaching'. It certainly does not depend upon the use of psychological jargon or the exposition of psychological concepts. It will rather be essentially Biblical and expository. But the Bible will be viewed in the perspective of (*a*) the real human condition of the congregation and (*b*) of the divine speaking to that condition which the Bible represents. Preaching will then begin to minister to the real questions agitating the minds of the hearers rather than the questions which they think they are asking or feel the minister is expecting them to ask.

Once a minister begins to embark upon this kind of preaching, he will see results almost immediately! They may not always be welcome to him! For some members of the congregation will inevitably react against sermons which touch sensitive areas of repressed mental pain. People do not willingly surrender their projection-laden images of God. They may be uncomfortable projections, but they have a cosy familiarity and they do serve the purpose of keeping the real God at bay. Other members of the congregation will begin to listen more intently to what the minister is saying, for they will sense a note of reality and authority in it arising from the preacher's real awareness of 'what is in man' (John 2.25). They may eventually be impelled to divest themselves of some of their masks and speak more freely of their real concerns to their fellow church members. In the process the congregation will start to attain to a level of fellowship ('sharing') at which Christ's promise of his presence with 'two or three gathered in his name' will really become meaningful.

As an instrument of theological education, however, the pulpit sermon is, of course, woefully inadequate. I quickly discovered this in my congregation at Stepney, where the practice at Sunday morning worship had been for the minister to preach a sermon to a small handful of eight to twelve people. The artificiality of the procedure had been evident to me for a long time. I felt that the very smallness of the congregation constituted an opportunity for far more effective preaching in terms of group discussion rather than in terms of the traditional sermon. But the biggest stumbling block in the way of breaking up the rigidity of the pattern of ministerial monologue was, I discovered, myself. I was afraid to let go the reins. I was also aware that some members of the congregation would feel easily threatened by the possibility of having their inarticulateness exposed in a group discussion.

One Sunday morning I ventured to appear in the pulpit wearing a collar and tie rather than the usual clerical collar. This modest effort at shattering the parsonic image led on to the initiation of 'group sermons'. I realized, as I preached the sermon that morning, that I had to come out of my pulpit. The following Sunday we began the experiment. Without any prior announcement we plunged into the deep end with a series of 'group sermons' for Lent on the main turning points in Jesus' ministry. Each member of the congregation was given a sheet listing the Bible passages to be read, if possible, beforehand. The sheet was headed with four reasons for preaching the sermon to each other: (i) To break down the barrier of silence between members of the congregation and the minister; (ii) To hear God addressing us in our speaking and listening together, gathered round his Word; (iii) To share frankly the questions that are important to *us* as members of the congregation, not merely to the minister; (iv) To imitate our Lord's example of instructing his disciples by dialogue and conversation.

After the initial shock the congregation quickly took advantage of their new freedom. In three out of the four sermons I led the discussion myself. On the one occasion on which a member of the congregation assumed this role the discussion went far better. The depth of insight into the Bible shown by the group went far beyond anything I had imagined possible. The very fact that we were also sharing insights into our human nature enhanced our understanding of the Bible, for, as one member of the group said, 'The Bible presents us with a mirror of ourselves'. I began to see my fellow members of the congregation in a new light. We surprised each other by the freshness of our thinking, and the opportunity to laugh in church was itself a source of great release for all of us.

We were fortunate, of course, in having a small modern building equipped with chairs which could be quickly formed into a circle. The very fact of sitting face to face was instrumental in forming new lines of communication between the members. We spoke to each other directly instead of through the minister alone. On that first morning we closed the sermon by sharing Holy Communion together seated literally around the communion table and passing the bread and wine from hand to hand.

This small experiment was satisfying because it both provided an experience of human encounter all too rare in the church, and an opportunity for interpreting that experience in terms of the Bible itself. This is more genuinely theological education than the one-sided pulpit utterance which is still the norm in most churches. At the same time it enabled me as minister to play my part as the theological specialist available to assist the group in its own thinking, without capitulating to the role of oracle which the group tried at first to impose upon me.

My own self-respect as a minister grew considerably as a

result of the 'group sermons'. For the first time I sensed the importance of my role as a theologian. This role is essentially an auxiliary one, through which the minister becomes available to the church as a 'resource-person' to assist his fellow-Christians in interpreting their own human experience in depth. I am proud to call myself a 'theologian', despite the suspicion of theology that is endemic amongst Anglo-Saxon Christians. Theological philistinism is not even confined to the laity. Many ministers are either not interested in theology, or are too hard-pressed by the clamour of 'church business' to continue their theological reading. Ministers often feel guilty about sitting down to read a theological book—understandably, for the introverted organizational church which they serve does not want them to be theologians. If the Church required its ministers to be theological specialists it would cease to clamour for 'more ministers' and ask rather for 'better-equipped ministers'. It would also realize that it is not necessary for every congregation to have its own resident theological specialist. With a more responsible laity and a stripped-down ecclesiastical plant in terms of fewer and more compact buildings, a minister could be deployed over a number of congregations as the full-time agent of theological training for the laity. Once he assumes his responsibilities as a theological specialist on behalf of the laity and their pastorate in the community, he will see many of his ecclesiastical chores to be entirely irrelevant. We may well take to heart the warning of Horst Symanowski, the German prophet of the Church in an industrialized society, when he writes:

The shoemaker has to stick to his last, the theologian to his theology. . . . [Theologians] are utterly misused today when they are set to tasks that are not within their province. These include not only administrative matters, such as construction of churches, nurseries, homes for the aged and parsonages. Things such as house calls, burials, and perhaps even baptism and other special acts usually associated with the pastoral office should also be included here. . . . The theologian should take himself seriously as a theologian.[4]

Ministers often make the excuse that 'my people are not interested in theology'. Such comments do little justice to the widespread latent interest in theology amongst lay-people, as I have discovered from my experience as a lecturer in 'new theology' at a local college of further education. A common reaction to these lectures is : 'Why can't we get this information from our own ministers?' Many laymen even express anger at having been denied, as they feel, the fruits of modern Biblical and theological scholarship. Many of my lectures have been attended by former churchgoers hungry for the theological insights with which the Church had failed to provide them. This is not to underestimate the zeal and sincerity shown by those ministers who value highly what is often called a 'teaching ministry'. But such teaching tends to be propositional in form, based as it often is upon, say, the articles of the Apostles' Creed. It tends, in other words, to start with God rather than man, and fails to take seriously the actual questions agitating the minds of its recipients.

The kind of theology most relevant to the needs of lay-people today has been described by the Bishop of Woolwich as 'opencast theology'. In an article written for *New Christian* he describes two ways of mining coal. The traditional method requires a great deal of plant both above and below the surface. The other method is that of 'opencast mining', in which the surface is excavated and eventually the top-soil put back and the land restored. There are correspondingly two ways of doing theology, both equally legitimate. The first way requires a great deal of plant in terms of university faculties of divinity, examinations, syllabuses, etc. It demands a great deal of training and its results are long-term in the extreme. The other method of

[4] H. Symanowski, *The Christian Witness in an Industrial Society*, Collins, 1966, p. 86.

'opencast theology' is described by the Bishop of Woolwich thus:

> Opencast theology starts its digging from much nearer the surface. It requires the minimum of plant and expensive machinery. It works on an open site with an invitation to any to join in. It demands the expertise of the professional, but in the capacity of resource-man to those whose starting-point is their own experience. It is not attempting to do the quarrying of rocks with which to build systems. But it has the advantage of beginning where people are and turning up the questions that arise beneath the surface of their own lives. And it moves on when those questions change.[5]

The pursuit of such theology is not easy for ministers who, like myself, were trained in a traditional theological college or seminary. I had, in fact, to unlearn most of the theology I had imbibed in the seminary, precisely because it was presented in terms of a closed ecclesiastical discipline. Nor did my 'practical' training help me to participate in the dialogue with others which is of the essence of 'opencast theology'. The sole concern of our homiletics classes was the preparation and delivery of pulpit sermons. There was no training in the leadership of a group discussion or in the theory of 'group dynamics'. A more serious lack, however, was the opportunity for gaining insight into the workings of a modern industrial society, such as is being provided in Germany by the six-month courses of the 'Seminar for the Church's Service in Industrial Society'.[6]

Unfortunately, 'opencast theology' is much more easily pursued by theologians who are not identified with the local congregation. It is almost impossible to develop a flexible theological approach in an almost static situation. My own theology came alive only in the setting of a team ministry in the East End of

[5] J. A. T. Robinson, 'Opencast Theology', *New Christian*, 15th June 1967, p. 13.
[6] See H. Symanowski, *op. cit.*, pp. 57 ff.

London where the institutional demands of a local congregation were almost at a minimum. Most of my time was, in fact, spent within secular agencies of one kind or another. Indeed I became so steeped in this atmosphere of open dialogue with the world that I made the mistake of thinking that the theological viewpoint thus engendered was that of the Church as a whole. I was rudely awakened, however, on those occasions when I addressed suburban churches on the theological issues posed by an East End ministry. Then I was met on the whole with blank incomprehension, and was disappointed to realize that the conditions for an 'opencast theology' were almost non-existent in most of our local congregations. My induction recently as minister of a fairly traditional local congregation has convinced me more than ever that the role of the minister as a theologian cannot be discussed apart from the question to which we now turn : 'What kind of Church?'

6

What Kind of Church?

THIS book began with a reference to the flight from the ordained ministry that is occurring in all the denominations today. I have tried to view this problem from the standpoint primarily of the men and women who serve the Church as ministers of local congregations. I have tried to suggest the proper role (as I see it) of the full-time ministry in a rapidly changing society. I have also stressed that this study of the task of the clergy is only one half of the picture. The real issue concerns the task of the whole Church as the people of God in the world, and the part to be played by the clergy in the fulfilment of that task. It will be evident from what I have said that the key to a renewed ministry (in the narrow, traditional sense of the ordained ministry) lies in the renewal of the whole Church for its mission in the world. Ultimately the Church gets only the ministers it deserves—and wants. As long as the Church sees ministers as ministering full-time on behalf of the sheep already in the fold, instead of assisting the Church in *its* pastorate (=mission) in the world, then the flight from the ministry will continue. Ministers of the younger generation, in particular, are becoming weary of labouring vicariously in the employ of congregations who have no vision of their apostolate. Hence the growing complaint of younger ministers that the ministry, conceived in terms of the average congregation's expectations of it, is not a man-size job today. This sense of the meaninglessness of so much ecclesiastical activity is only highlighted by the activism and neurotic 'busyness' of the average parson. They represent the attempt to quell the nagging suspicion that there is not much point to the traditional clerical activity anyway. However, because of the thraldom of the institution binding both minister and congregation in a highly collusive relationship of mutual guilt and evasion of reality, few ministers are able both to struggle free of the 'rat-race' and to remain within the ordained ministry. This is a tragedy. For the key to a renewed ministry does not lie in flight from the full-time ministry but in the formation of a body of clergy who are prepared to remain within it while resisting the stultifying pressures of the institution. Such clergy must be prophets in the true sense, able to discern the demonic 'principalities and powers' (particularly ecclesiastical ones) and to declare them vanquished in the name of him who on the Cross 'discarded the cosmic powers and authorities like a garment, . . . made a public spectacle of them and led them as captives in his triumphal procession' (Col. 2.15 NEB).

Having said this, I must go on to say that many more ministers will have to leave the full-time 'pastorate' before the stage is set for renewal. The kind of ministry I have sketched in this book requires a clarity of vision and the development of skills not provided or required by the traditional round of church life. The current cry for 'more clergy' is misplaced if they are intended merely to keep a dying institution propped up. Today we need, in fact, fewer but better deployed and more specialized clergy with a specific part to play in the total ministry of the Church. As prophets they will point the Church to its concern with the world, not itself. As pastors, they will be training and guiding the laity in *their* pastorate. As theologians they will be equipping the Church to reflect meaningfully upon God's activity in an increasingly secularized society. To find men and women capable of fulfilling such responsibilities will not be easy. For any training for a ministry of this kind will be rigorous in the extreme, as we can see if we review the three tasks of prophet, pastor and theologian in turn.

The *prophet* needs to have a very clear perception of the forces moulding society at large. He will not need to know intimately every aspect of society. That would be impossible in an increasingly pluriform community. He will need, however, to have direct knowledge of one or two of the major institutions shaping our common life today. Whether he acquires such knowledge before ordination or after it does not matter. In any event the Church must provide him with facilities for gaining experience of this kind, even if it means seconding him to a 'secular' institution for a lengthy period of time. No minister concerned to sharpen his awareness of the 'principalities and powers' could fail to benefit from direct participation in, say, industry or one of the social services.

Training for the *pastorate* has already been dealt with at length in this book. The Church can no longer afford to treat with suspicion and downright anxiety the field of psychotherapy which has so much to offer in the shape of tools for an effective pastorate. It is, of course, obvious that not every ordinand or minister will be able to stand the rigours of training in this field. It is the experience of those running courses in psychotherapy for general practitioners, as well as for clergy, that there is quite a serious 'drop-out' rate from such courses as a result of the anxieties they arouse in the participants. This is quite understandable in view of the limited though significant changes in personality that these courses can induce. Nobody can be blamed for these failures to 'finish the course', least of all the ministers concerned. But one must ask again whether the inability to accept the insight that training in psychotherapy brings with it is not a disqualification for the pastoral ministry, as it is, for example, for participation in the field of social casework. The only alternative to providing every minister with these tools is to develop team ministries in which those not equipped for this kind of pastoral care in depth work alongside those who are so equipped. This sounds well in theory, but founders on the fact that psychological insight which unlocks the door to a minister's inner life is a necessary basis for both prophetic and theological insight. Without it the ministry will suffer on every, not simply the pastoral, level.

There is a sense in which the minister's training as a *theologian* cannot be separated from the kind of training I have outlined above. My contention throughout has been that the proper context for theological training is direct involvement in some form of 'secular' discipline such as will provide the kind of 'disclosure situation' from which theological insight grows. It is doubtful whether the traditional theological college can offer such situations, orientated as they are to the study of theology as a separate 'book-discipline'. There are signs of hope in this field, however. Attempts at a more relevant type of theological training are being made in British universities, e.g. Bristol and Birmingham, but such enterprise is less obvious in the theological colleges as such. In my own denomination there has been for some years a rather tenuous link between our theological college in Cambridge and a small urban training centre in the East End of London. Theological students have resided at this centre during their vacations and participated in a type of ministry far removed from that of the typical 'gathered congregation'. Nevertheless, such participation has always been rated a very low priority in the theological curriculum at this college, which ensures that every student is seconded for a number of vacations to work under ministers of 'more typical' local congregations. The limitation thus placed upon the student's exposure to the problems of inner urban areas, from which my own denomination has been retreating over many decades, is an inevitable result of the Church's fixation upon the residential congregation as the norm of all ministry. A relevant theological training presupposes a Church which is ready and willing to scrutinize its present structures and ask whether they are really an adequate context for fulfilment of the kind of dynamic, responsive and responsible ministry I have been describing.

At the moment, the local parish or congregation is regarded as the norm of all ministry. As an instrument of mission it is proving, through no fault of its own, less and less effective. Yet it clamours more and more frantically for the exclusive services of expensively trained and maintained full-time ministers. It can only finance such a ministry by laying ever heavier burdens of money raising upon a declining membership—this despite the growing success of stewardship campaigns. The signs are out that, at least in my own denomination, the limits of financial capacity are being reached. On economic grounds, therefore, the traditional pattern of 'one minister, one congregation', is doomed. Attempts to group congregations under one minister generally prove unsuccessful, for the perpetuation of obsolete demands upon the minister tend to run him into the ground through sheer exhaustion. Even 'team-ministries' involving a few ministers serving one church on a collegiate basis, or a number of churches on a group basis, still perpetuate the pattern of an exclusive relationship between the local residence-based congregations and the theological specialists. They also encounter the added hazard of the 'team' becoming an autonomous clerical enclave *vis-à-vis* the laity.

A proper acceptance of the minister's role as a theological specialist must cut the nerve of the Church's fixation upon the local congregation as the norm of all ministry. For the minister will then be seen as free to train the laity for mission in other equally legitimate church groups or 'ecclesial forms', e.g. vocational groups, house churches, urban training centres, industrial missions, etc. This spreading of responsibility for mission over a number of agencies does not mean the abolition of the local congregation, as Harvey Cox points out:

The difficulty is that we are not moving from one stage of society in which a particular form of church life, the residential parish, was the characteristic form into a stage in which some other form of church life will replace it. The situation is far more complex. The key word to describe what is happening in our society is *differentiation*. We are moving into a stage in which we will need a widely differentiated range of different types of church organization to engage a society which is becoming differentiated at an accelerated rate. Church life in the secular metropolis will certainly include congregations based on residence, but since residence . . . touches people today in only one segment of their lives, we shall also need other forms of church life *alongside* it. Not only will future forms of church life be differentiated and specialized, they must also be flexible and disposable, ready in their turn to give way to newer forms.

The Church must be ready for differentiation if it wants to exist in a rapidly differentiating society. Defenders of the parish church would do better to see what it can realistically be expected to do in an industrial-urban setting instead of defending it against all critics. The truth is that the parish *can* do certain things, but it cannot do some of the things which must be accomplished by industrial missions, lay academies and issue-orientated groupings. Attackers of the residence parish, on their side, had best realize that imprecations will not kill social institutions. Much wealth and talent and leadership is still concentrated in residential parishes and will be for some time. The real question is how this fund of resources can be channelled into a ministry of exorcism in the city.[1]

Cox's warning against easy dismissal of the congregation-based ministry in a parish setting is salutary. What such ministry needs is not *abolition* but *renewal*, a liberation into responsibility for specific though limited aims in connection with the life of family, home and the needs of the more static sections of the population, notably children and old people. Such renewal will only come when the parish church is fanned by the fresh breeze of reality blowing from other sectors of the Christian frontier, particularly those impinging on the broader institutions, indus-

[1] Harvey Cox, *The Secular City*, SCM Press, 1965, pp. 157 f.

try, commerce, the mass-media, education and government, which are moulding the family setting and helping to create the domestic problems which hitherto the parish church has tried to solve in isolation.

One of the main hindrances, however, to the renewal of the local congregation at the present time lies in the widespread loss of morale in the Church caused by the shattering decline, attested annually by the reports of denominational general secretaries, in the number of church members. There is no evidence to suggest that this decline will be in any way halted in the foreseeable future. Today we are witnessing the literal break-up of the institutional church in the form in which it has existed for centuries. This break-up is the result, as we have already noted, of vast changes in social patterns which have made the local church almost completely irrelevant to the needs of our highly mobile and increasingly anonymous society. Because the Church has always depended on the *status quo* economically and socially, it is dangerously vulnerable to changes in its environment. This vulnerability was less apparent in the days when social and economic change was slow, but has become glaringly apparent in these days when, as Harvey Cox has reminded us, rapid social change is simply a euphemism for 'revolution'.[2]

My concern, however, at this point is not to diagnose the causes of decline, but to ask the question: in what sense do numbers matter in the Church? We can only answer this question by reflecting upon the whole *raison d'être* of the Church, what it exists to do and to be, in the light of the Bible itself. There we find few grounds for concluding that the Church was ever intended to be a majority movement. Such a conclusion runs counter to the nature of the Gospel, which has always had a minority appeal. The assumption behind much of the Church's 'evangelism', however, is that the Gospel is capable of being

[2] *Op. cit.*, p. 107.

accepted by the many rather than the few. The Church is right in that assumption if it means that the privilege of response to the Gospel is not granted to any particular section of humanity, but is available to all, rich and poor, clever or simple, old or young alike. The Gospel is indeed universal in its scope. But it is by no means universal in its appeal. When we consider the in-built resistance to acceptance of the freedom of the Gospel such as I have referred to in this book, resistances which are by no means the monopoly of non-churchgoers or 'non-Christians', it is hardly surprising that very few people in fact discover what it is essentially about.

Harry Williams makes this point tellingly in *Objections to Christian Belief*:

'Straight is the gate and narrow is the way', said Jesus, 'which leadeth unto life, and few there be that find it.' The churches generally preach something different—'Few there be who, having found it, have the moral courage to walk on it or remain walking on it. For it is easy enough to find. It is plain for all to see.' The ease and certainty with which the churches point to the road and their assumption that it is obvious to all men of good will leads me to think that the road they thus recommend is not the narrow way at all but the wide gate and the broad way which leads to destruction.[3]

Here my own thinking has been much influenced by experience of a minority situation in East London, where the proportion of churchgoers in the population is lower possibly than anywhere else in the country. But the proportion of those who have made a genuine response to the Gospel in terms of the inner freedom it bestows is certainly no different here from anywhere else. Such a statement might appear to be arrogant, in that it seems to postulate the existence of a small spiritual élite

[3] H. A. Williams, 'Psychological Objections' in *Objections to Christian Belief*, Constable, 1963 (cited from the edition published by Penguin Books, 1965, p. 42).

who have been initiated into a modern version of an ancient 'mystery-religion'. Such arrogance, however, would be a total denial of all that the small representative body of believers exists to do, i.e. to fulfil its vocation as servants of the many. In this connection I acknowledge a debt to Hans-Ruedi Weber of the Ecumenical Institute, Bossey, Switzerland, for an article he wrote in *Frontier* entitled 'God's Arithmetic'. The article first struck me with the force of a revelation, and I have continually adjusted my sights by it ever since.

Weber begins by quoting a conversation about evangelism which he had in California with a group of keen Lutheran laymen and pastors who were planning the excellent evangelism project for the San Fernando Valley :

'What will happen if we plan our evangelism project according to the insights we have now gained?' 'Frankly, it may be that many among your present church-membership will leave the Church and that a few who are now completely outside the Church will join you.' 'You mean to say that as a result of this project we may in the end actually be fewer !'

Weber continues :

In the course of our conversation we were led to that staggering discovery, which none of us was quite ready to accept, namely that the result of true evangelism may be the cutting down of the number of church-members. Evangelism and outward church-growth will not necessarily go together.

Of course, it is often said that 'quality matters more than quantity' where church membership is concerned. But I get the impression that this statement is often made in an attempt to rationalize disappointment over lack of numerical 'success'. It also begs the question of what exactly we mean by 'quality'; in other words it leads us back to, but does not answer the question : why does the Church exist at all?

Numbers, of course, can never be the point of departure for

D

consideration of this question. Our point of departure must be the Bible which, as Weber says, 'reveals some astonishing things which are a paradox to our mathematical minds'. He points out that God's strategy as revealed in the Bible is that to achieve the salvation of all he elects, calls and converts a *few*. Abraham is the prototype of the one man, God's man, who was to bring crisis and benediction to all (Gen. 12.2). 'Yet the history of Israel is no success story. Sometimes the numerical growth and outward strength actually hindered Israel from being God's people.' Only when Gideon's army was cut down from 32,000 to 300 'was it ready to fight God's battle' (Judg. 7).

Weber points out that the same paradox is to be seen in the New Testament. 'In order to save the *cosmos* God sends the One, his own Son. Christ calls a few, the representative twelve, and he sends them into the whole inhabited world to be witnesses of his cosmic redemption.'

Weber concludes :

Numbers and growth are important in God's arithmetic : not necessarily large and increasing numbers but representative numbers and growth in grace. The representative few stand for all. Their mission consists not in propaganda in order that many may be induced to become like the few. Rather it consists in being *pars pro toto*, the part standing for the whole, being the light of the *cosmos*, salt of the earth, good seed sown in the field of the world. The key question is not how churches can grow numerically, but how they can grow in grace and so become God's representative number. . . . Church history would seem to suggest that growth in maturity often fosters growth in minority church situations while in majority situations it often brings about a healthy diminution of church membership, because many nominal Christians discover the cost of discipleship. We must leave the matter of statistics to God and concentrate all our energy on discerning and serving God's cosmic mission of reconciliation.[4]

[4] H.-R. Weber, 'God's Arithmetic', *Frontier*, Winter 1963, Vol. 6, No. IV, pp. 298 ff.

We must face the fact, then, that faithfulness to its vocation may inevitably lead to a reduction in numbers. This may indeed be a surprising consequence of evangelism but, as Weber has made clear, there is good Biblical warrant for this conclusion. Above all, Jesus himself declared time and again that the call to discipleship, though addressed to all, would be answered only by a few. This does not mean that the few will become a kind of 'in-group'. Such thinking leads to the mentality of the ghetto, and the ghetto is essentially a group defensive against the world rather than existing for the world. The important thing about the Church is that, large or small, it exists in an attitude of openness to the world. A new term has been coined by theologians to describe this relationship of the Church to the world—'pro-existence'. Pro-existence means existing for the world, on behalf of the world, for the welfare of the world.

J. A. T. Robinson develops this theme of 'pro-existence' in his book *The New Reformation?* He draws a distinction (drawn originally by Paul Tillich) between the 'manifest Church', when Christ is consciously recognized and worshipped, and the 'latent Church', to which those belong who do not consciously acknowledge Christ, but whose whole relationship to the world is implicitly if not explicitly Christ-like. He asks:

What then is the function of the manifest Church in the new Reformation? I suggest that it is not there primarily as the organized centre *into* which to draw men—as if the enlarging of this circle were the object of the whole exercise. It is indeed the dedicated nucleus of those who actively acknowledge Jesus as Lord and have committed themselves to membership and mission within the visible sacramental fellowship of the Spirit. Yet its *normal* form of existence, when it is distinctively being itself, is *not* to be gathered together in one place, but to be embedded as seeds of light within the dark world.[5]

Acceptance of this view of the Church as the representative

[5] J. A. T. Robinson, *The New Reformation?*, SCM Press, 1965, p. 48.

few existing for the sake of the many must lead to a revaluation of all aspects of the Church's life. For far too much energy is still being expended on gathering people into the Church as if the boundaries of the Church were co-terminous with the Kingdom of God. It is becoming increasingly apparent to Christians working in 'frontier situations' that the Church exists not as the *goal* of mission but as the *agent* of mission. By this token a member of the Church is (*a*) one who has seen for himself what is true for all men, namely, God's acceptance of the world as declared normatively in Jesus Christ, (*b*) pledges himself to declare with the rest of the Church the truth of God's acceptance, and (*c*) spreads the contagion of that freedom from the past and that openness to the future which is a genuine Gospel-event whether it leads to the declaration 'Christ is Lord' or not.

So many current practices of the Church would need revising in the light of such a definition of church membership. Infant baptism, for example, would appear to be called seriously into question when viewed in the light of the Church's role as the few existing for the many. At present the practice of infant baptism is fraught with contradictions. As a declaration of God's initiative in redeeming all men it is, of course, unexceptionable. But in the New Testament baptism combines the declaration of God's grace with a conscious response to it on the part of the believer. It is the point at which the believer testifies to the awareness of his freedom as a son of God and identifies himself with the Church as the community committed to mediating that same awareness to the world. No such response is possible in the case of infant baptism. A case might be argued, of course, for retaining infant baptism as an expression of the first half of the equation: God's gracious initiative, if not of the second half: the believer's response to that initiative. In that case, the Church ought logically to baptize infants with no strings or conditions attached, simply as a declaration of what is true for all men whether they respond or not. My own practice with regard to infant baptism reflects this view of the sacrament. Over the years I have become less and less inclined to stress to parents the conditions on which the Church baptizes children. I am still haunted by the memory of one tearful mother to whom I once refused the baptism of her new-born child because of a failure to send the older children to Sunday school. I vowed that I would never allow such a thing to happen again, although I continued to feel guilty about baptizing the children of non-members of the congregation. My feelings on baptism changed considerably when I began to reappraise the significance of the fact that I had been baptized in infancy. At moments of intense personal crisis I began to reflect more and more upon the fact of my baptism, like Luther who, under stress of dire temptation, scrawled the words upon his desk 'baptizatus sum'. I began to realize the possibilities of infant baptism as the declaration of God's acceptance of me for what I was rather than for what I could do to justify my own existence. I could thus reappropriate my baptism at the point where I became conscious of my vocation as a Christian believer. On such grounds I would hesitate to abolish infant baptism as such, although as the public demand for infant baptism declines the practice of believers' baptism will grow in importance.

The real problem concerns not the sacraments as such or their mode of administration but the context in which they are celebrated. Every baptism implies a declaration of intent on the part of the Church to be a community which embodies the realities of the sacrament within its own life. If baptism declares God's acceptance of us in Jesus Christ, then the Church must be the 'accepting community' *par excellence*. That the Church tends to be anything but such an accepting community is all too obvious. If baptism declares the Church's commitment to the world as the sphere of God's activity, then the Church which is self-regarding and introverted will be playing the hypocrite in baptizing at all. As it is, discerning Christians are increasingly confessing the unreality for them of worship and the sacraments, particularly the sacrament of Holy Communion, precisely, so I believe, because of the impoverishment of their setting. This was brought home to me recently at a lay-training conference when a Presbyterian elder of many years standing professed, with a sense of guilt, that he 'got nothing out of Holy Communion at all'. It turned out that nearly all the members of the group felt the same. The Communion as observed in their own local congregations meant very little to them. Their complaint, however, was not with the sacrament as such, for several of them recalled occasions when it had been meaningful, notably at small weekend conferences. Then there had been a quality of sharing at a deeper level for which the sacrament had provided a significant endorsement. This was precisely our experience in Stepney after the group sermons when, as I described in the last chapter, we celebrated Holy Communion seated round the Table, passing the bread and wine from hand to hand. The sacrament became a 'celebration', an act of rejoicing in God's acceptance of the world as made real to us by the accepting quality of the group itself. This truth of the sacrament came home to me even more forcibly at one of the housegroups to which I referred in Chapter 4, a group divided equally between churchgoers and non-churchgoers. A day arrived when we felt able to celebrate Holy Communion together seated in the front parlour of a condemned East End near-slum dwelling. On this occasion we shared a bottle of ordinary wine bought from the local wine store and toasted each other with wine glasses instead of passing a cup from hand to hand. Afterwards we shared the remaining contents of the bottle together, and departed realizing, for the first time, what 'eucharist' really meant.

In his book, *God's Grace in History*, written before his departure from the Roman Catholic priesthood, Charles Davis has pinpointed the weakness of current eucharistic practice in the fact that the Church lacks an adequate structure of 'primary groups' in which there can be intimate face-to-face association and co-operation. Such groups are all the more necessary in a secular society which places a premium upon the Christian's possession of a free, personal faith. There is a danger, however, of the believer being left in isolation unless primary groups of Christians are formed to provide him with support. The urban parish, because of its size, is necessarily a secondary group, which he defines as 'a wider association not resting upon immediate personal encounter, but held together by common beliefs and values, by the expression of these in language and symbol, and by a unity of administration'.[6] Davis argues that the Eucharist belongs more properly to the secondary than to the primary group level. 'The chief function of the Eucharist is to unite and express the full community of the Church. It does not just seal the intimacy of those already united by personal association.'[7] There is room for discussion on this point. Many theologians today believe that the Eucharist must now take its place with the primary, rather than the secondary group. But Davis's point concerning the necessity for primary groups is incontestable, for without them there will be little reality in the Eucharist.

There is no limit to the possibilities for change and experiment in worship and sacrament once the Church begins to take seriously its representative function as a community committed to 'pro-existence' on behalf of the world. Perhaps the saving thing about the massive decline in the Church's members, in England at least, is that Christians are now being forced to ask about the nature of the Church in the absence of any great numerical 'strength'. It appears that only by thus being 'brought to its knees' will the Church begin to ask such questions. Unfortunately, obsolete structures have a habit of stifling the growth of more dynamic expressions of faith, one of them being the

[6] Charles Davis, *God's Grace in History*, Fontana Books, Collins, 1966, p. 68.
[7] *Op. cit.*, p. 69.

ordained ministry conceived of as a separate clerical caste. I have already discussed some of the psychological factors which prevent the abolition of the 'clergy-line'. These are not the only factors at work, however. Another barrier to a change in the relationship of clergy and laity is constituted by the traditional practice of ordination, to which we now turn.

Fresh thinking within the Church on any subject has usually a very minor influence upon its actual practice, especially where the changes required are of a liturgical character. Where such changes fail to be effected, the climate of resistance to fresh thinking is perpetuated for a very long time after the new ideas have received tacit if not explicit acceptance within the Church. The old tag *lex orandi lex credendi* (the law of prayer is the law of belief) holds true especially in the matter of ordination. As long as ordination services continue to reflect a discredited view of the ministry, so long will it take the generality of church members to see and accept the point of our rediscovered emphasis upon the apostolate of the laity.

It is understandable, though deplorable, that those Christian communions which are tied, as is the Church of England, to old liturgical forms should have the greatest difficulty in giving practical expression to new theological insights. The Church of England's 1662 service for the 'Ordering of Priests' presents, as can be expected, the typical picture of the priest delivering the whole thrust of Christ's ministry to the world, rather than as embodying prophetically what is essentially the ministry of the whole 'laos' of God to the world. So the Bishop's charge to the candidate reads in the archaic phraseology of the Prayer Book :

And now again we exhort you, in the name of our Lord Jesus Christ, that you have in remembrance, into how high a dignity, and to how weighty an office and charge ye are called : that is to say, to be messengers, watchmen and stewards of the Lord; to teach, and to premonish, to feed and provide for the Lord's family; to seek for Christ's sheep that are dispersed abroad, and for his children who are in the midst of this naughty world, that they may be saved through Christ for ever.

The monarchical conception of the ministry presupposed in this exhortation is still reflected in modern formularies, not least in those of my own communion. In the 'Form and Order for the Ordination and Induction of Ministers' of the Presbyterian Church of England, the *ethos* of the ministry conveyed in the ordination prayer is essentially that of the solitary pastor serving a group of people who are there to support him in *his* ministry:

Enable him to fulfil his ministry among this people, breaking to them the bread of life, tending the young of the flock, comforting the burdened and sorrowful, and so ministering the grace of God that this congregation may be a healing and reconciling community in the place in which it is set.

The reference to the congregation as a 'healing and reconciling community' does hint at a shift of emphasis from the sole apostolate of the minister to that of the whole congregation, and is to be welcomed. But this note needs to be sounded much more firmly, especially in view of the constant gravitational pull of the traditional and quite unbiblical conception of the minister as the sole vehicle of ministry. Thus one of the questions put to the congregation by the Moderator of Presbytery before the act of ordination still perpetuates the image of the minister as the father-figure requiring to be backed up by the congregation:

Do you, the members and adherents of this congregation, in accepting the minister whom you have called, promise him all dutiful respect, encouragement, support and obedience in the Lord?

The tragedy is that this exaltation of the office of the 'ordained ministry' only serves to depreciate the ministry of the laity as a whole. Yet it is this latter ministry which alone justifies the existence of an ordained ministry, for only as a theological resource for the apostolate of the laity can the minister be seen as having any part to play at all.

It is not my intention to embark upon a discussion of the various views of ordination current within the major Christian communions. Such a discussion would not impinge upon the basic problem with which we are here concerned, namely the identification of 'orders' with the status and functions of a separate clerical caste. In *The New Reformation?* J. A. T. Robinson points out that the 'clergy-line' is neither native nor essential to the Church:

It is indeed an alien importation, introduced from the difference between the *plebs* and the *ordo*, the commons and the senate, in the administrative machinery of the Roman Empire. It was entrenched in the Church at the time of its establishment under Constantine, when it became necessary to define the rights and benefits of clergy transferred to it from the heathen priesthood. I believe the whole thing could disappear without loss, together with the medieval concept of indelibility, the mystique, the status, the theology and the legalities by which it has been buttressed and surrounded in our various traditions. The whole differentiation implied in the terms '*sacred* ministry' and '*holy* orders' is one that is now destructive of rather than constructive of the Body of Christ.[8]

We must note that John Robinson is not dismissing ordination as such, but simply its identification with the clergy-line. In fact, he points out in another context that, by the 'clergy-line' he does not mean 'the entirely proper distinctions within the life of the Body between the liturgies and functions of different orders and members—Bishops, Presbyters, Deacons, Readers, Catechists, etc.'.[9] For all of the multiplicity of possible ministries within the Church it would be proper to have some form of ordination. The term 'ordination' would then be freed for use as

---

[8] J. A. T. Robinson, *op. cit.*, p. 57.
[9] J. A. T. Robinson, *Meeting, Membership and Ministry*, Prism Pamphlet No. 31, 1966, pp. 12 f.

a description of whatever kind of authorization the Church deemed necessary for any particular ministry. The essence of ordination would then be its function as an authorization of what are *all* 'lay-ministries', in that they are all ministries within the total 'laos' or 'people of God'.

One aspect of traditional ordination theory remains still to be mentioned : ordination as a vehicle of the Church's continuity. The part played by ordination in the perpetuation of the clergy-line has been to a great extent the part that it has played as a symbol of the transmission of apostolic authority from one generation to another. This, more than anything else, has, particularly in the episcopal communions, resulted in a massive cleavage between 'clergy' and 'laity'. The possessor of 'orders' inevitably came to assume a status within the Church far outweighing that of the 'layman', for the Church could be the Church without the latter but not without the former.

Ordination as a vehicle for the transmission of apostolic authority inevitably stands or falls by the view one takes of the whole nature of the Church and its continuity. It would be pointless here to enter upon a discussion of apostolic succession, except to say that those who uphold the traditional view of such succession in terms of an unbroken chain of authority secured by the laying on of hands back to apostolic times, will tend to hold a view of ordination difficult to reconcile with the more functional view of ordination that I have described. Ordination as a means of ensuring continuity of authority within the Church means little to me. I can, however, see some point in ordination as a witness to the Church's commitment to its total apostolic ministry in the world. Ordination in this sense would not ensure the Church's claim to be an apostolic community. It would have rather to be justified by evidence on other grounds that the Church is committed to this apostolate. An introverted clericalized 'church' could in no sense justify its claim to be the Church on the strength of possessing an apparently intact 'apostolic succession' in the traditional sense. The only continuity the Church dare claim is the continuity of its commitment to its apostolate, which apostolate must be continually renewed and confirmed at every point in the Church's life. Ordination as a sign of this commitment has its proper place. Nevertheless ordination, as it is commonly practised by the main Christian denominations, tends to veil this commitment on the grounds that I have already adduced, namely that it tends to be upheld at the expense of rather than in support of the apostolate of the whole 'laos' and that it has become identified with a 'professional' view of the ordained ministry, which isolates it conspicuously from the real pressures and problems faced by the members of the Church who follow other occupations. John Robinson suggests a way of remedying these objections to current ordination practice when he writes:

I should wish to question . . . whether ordination in any of our churches should ever include a built-in guarantee of £1,000 a year for life (or whatever is its equivalent). Ordination means the commissioning of a man for a particular order or function of ministry within the Body of Christ. It need not of itself imply any undertaking that he is to be taken on the pay-roll of the Church or will remain on it. The Church should remain entirely free in this matter, and make it clear from the beginning that ordination is a calling and not necessarily a profession.[10]

The 'deprofessionalizing' of the ordained ministry in this sense will accomplish little, however, if it fails to reflect a complete reorientation of the relationship between the clergy and the rest of the laity. Those denominations which make great use of 'part-time ministers', particularly the Congregational and Baptist Churches, do not seem to be noticeably less clericalized than my own. Such clericalism betrays a remarkable insensitivity to the changes in attitudes to authority which are occurring in all spheres of society today. It is here that we come, I believe, to the

[10] J. A. T. Robinson, *The New Reformation?*, p. 58.

nub of the problem of ordination. Basically this problem is not theological but sociological. In the matter of ordination, as in so many other matters, the Church has succeeded in rationalizing a secular problem into an ecclesiastical one. The kind of clericalism made respectable by monarchical views of ordination simply reflects the outmoded and inadequate conception of authority which is coming under fire in all areas of society at the present time.

It is a platitude to say that we are living in an anti-authoritarian age. To many people such anti-authoritarianism constitutes a decadence which heralds the end virtually of civilization. To others, however, the rebellion against traditional authority in any form is a symptom of the search for the only worthwhile kind of authority, namely that which is non-coercive and deeply respectful of people's freedom to accept or reject it. It is not only the Church which is experiencing a revolt against the old 'authorities'. In the academic world, particularly, such revolt is now commonplace. Students no longer accept their teachers as standing *in loco parentis*, especially when such parental authority is exercised patronizingly and insensitively. The now famous student riots at the University of Berkeley, California, and the London School of Economics, ran true to the pattern of contemporary rejection of authoritarian attitudes of all kinds.

In Chapter 2 I have already discussed the dynamics of authoritarianism affecting the relationship between minister and congregation. On the level of practical training for the ministry the emphasis must be placed in this anti-authoritarian age upon the role of the minister within a 'peer-group' rather than a 'dependent group'. Any minister who tries to create such a peergroup structure within his congregation will find, as I found, the mystique surrounding his orders quickly dispelled. At the same time he will find the traditional concepts and practices associated with ordination a serious hindrance to creating the structure of a peer-group. The clerical collar, for example, is a grievous stumbling block in a church which is striving for genuine mutuality in its relationships.

Originally, so I believe, the clerical collar was a symbol of servanthood. Now it has become the symbol of authoritarianism, an article of dress which aligns the minister unmistakably in most people's minds with the 'establishment'. Having almost entirely given up the clerical collar, I am finding a greatly enhanced freedom to developing mutual relationships with others. But the problem goes deeper than can be solved by a simple rejection of the clerical collar. Authoritarianism is not the monopoly of the clergy. Nor are they the sole obstacle to the growth of the Church into a mutual community. Much of the resistance to the minister's surrender of authoritarian attitudes stems from the laity for reasons adduced in Chapter 2. Nevertheless, the problem is not purely a psychological one. Ultimately it is theological in so far as it raises the question : how are men and women to be liberated from their old dependencies into the freedom to be there for others, as Christ was. The answer comes in terms of Gethsemane and the Cross. For growth in love, which is what we are really talking about, involves suffering as we submit to the pain of being exposed, defenceless and vulnerable, within the world and that mysterious community of redemption known as the Church. It is with the nature of this suffering in relation to the minister that we must now deal.

7

A Fool for Christ

THE original inspiration for this book derived from the wish
to explain to myself, as much as to anyone else, why I remained
in the ministry at the point where I had the clearest opportunity
and inclination to leave it. In the Introduction I have already
suggested some reasons for my continuing to be a minister. I
cannot leave this discussion of 'a ministry renewed' without
examining a little further the compulsion laid upon me to
remain within the ordained ministry, meaning, in this context,
the parochial ministry.

It will be apparent to those who have read this far that I am
something of a rebel. There is plenty of material for such rebellion in the ministry as it is at present constituted. It is almost
too easy for any radical Christian to criticize the Church today.
More traditional Christians are accustomed to being scolded by
radicals impatient for reform. The scolding goes on in both
directions and results in a complete breakdown of communication on both sides of the radical divide. It is partly because I wish
to keep the lines of communication open that I have remained
in the parochial ministry. The debate must not be allowed to
polarize entirely between those who continue as ministers and
those who have given up the ministry. The reminder has been
made, perhaps more often by radicals than by traditionalists,
that radicals and traditionalists need each other. Many ministers,
of whom I am one, feel it their responsibility to remain within

the institution and 'kick like hell'. This does not necessarily mean being a frustrated minister. Far too often it is argued by traditionalists: if these ministers are so frustrated why don't they get out? I do not consider myself as basically a frustrated minister, although there are frustrations in plenty! Chronic frustration is rooted in a lack of assurance concerning the Gospel. It is also compounded of a great deal of guilt at wanting to leave the ministry and yet needing its support at the same time. Such frustration is uncreative and impotent. The true radical, though aware of and experiencing frustration, is possessed of an assurance which undergirds his attack upon the corruption of the institution. This assurance springs from an experience of the Gospel as true. It is the lack of this experience and of opportunities for gaining it that I have criticized so frequently in this book. The Christian has no fear of change when he knows his acceptance in Jesus Christ. The security which this acceptance engenders provides the only possible springboard for change within the Church. It no longer has a vested interest in the past, when its grounds for hope lie in Christ who is the Lord of the future. The theologians of renewal have been wrongly criticized for wishing merely to be fashionable. The very word 'renewal' springs from a profound understanding and awareness of the power of Christ to 'make all things new'. Renewal is rooted in the reality of death and resurrection which is the heart of the Gospel. Merely to be fashionable, however, is to attempt to change without repentance. It is inevitably superficial and ineffective, for it evades the necessity for that total reorientation of ourselves which is of the essence of repentance.

But my rebellion is not directed only at the traditionalists. There is a certain kind of radical towards whom I also react rebelliously. He is the radical who is intent on sweeping away the ordained ministry as totally absurd and irrelevant in contemporary society. In this book I have adduced many grounds for agreeing with him almost entirely. In the age of the 'peer group' it is almost impossible to justify the continuance of an office as loaded with false presuppositions about authority as the ministry. In a plural society, the traditional idea of the 'parson' as the 'persona' or representative person in the community has died. In an age of specialists, the idea of the minister as possessing some significance for the whole of human experience rings no bells at all. In the age of the 'laity', the idea of the ministry performing a vicarious apostolate on behalf of the whole Church is rightly discredited. Yet there remains within me a stubborn refusal to surrender the ministry altogether. I have felt this all the more strongly since my induction as the minister of a congregation consisting partly of scientists at an atomic energy research establishment. Many of these scientists are deeply radical in their beliefs and are witnessing at the very centre of the technological revolution. My present physical isolation in a remote country village, to which my congregation repairs from miles around by car on Sundays only to disappear almost totally for another seven days, has only served to emphasize my remoteness as a minister from the day-to-day concerns of the rest of the laity. My initial reaction to this situation was to regret that I had not left the ministry after all. The fact that some of my congregation are more competent theologically than I am only intensified my sense of redundancy. My immediate inclination in these circumstances was to find a part-time 'secular' job which would at least ensure some regular contact with non-churchgoers who, after all, do make up the majority of the British population. The inclination began to fade, however, when I sensed that my congregation were looking in the minister for something other than a pale imitation of themselves. The very fact that they invested some physical and emotional capital in travelling thirty miles, in some cases, to worship in an isolated Presbyterian church testified, however inarticulately, to a need for the opportunity to reflect upon the significance of their daily preoccupations. They needed to be reminded that the 'principalities and powers' which shape the lives of all of us have been vanquished in Jesus Christ. The very absurdity, in fact, of the minister's role today is precisely its strength rather than its weakness. It constitutes a reminder that the world needs, in a sense, to take itself less seriously, in the light of the absurd but glorious fact that God loves it and is redeeming it.

This positive view of the minister's absurdity came home to me as the result of reading an article entitled 'Letter on the Parish Ministry' by Peter L. Berger.[1] In this letter to an ordinand Berger attempts to answer the question whether the parish ministry today is not 'irrelevant', 'ineffective', 'morally ambiguous' and 'generally absurd'. He begins by replying to all these charges in the affirmative and goes on to examine the deeper implications of his affirmative answers. He points out that the ministry certainly has no monopoly of irrelevance, ineffectiveness, moral ambiguity and absurdity. Other professions are loaded with precisely the same handicaps, and it would be unrealistic to forget that, despite the high expectations people have of the ministry, it is not a 'sacrosanct vocation, exempt from the ordinary pressures that other men are exposed to'. With this judgment I concur, the more so as a result of meeting members of other professions, notably medicine and social work, and discovering that their problems are very akin to those of the ministry. In particular, the division between radicals and traditionalists, though not so entrenched perhaps as in the Church, is a source of conflict and frustration in those professions. Questions of declining status, allied with a falling standard of living, have led to grievous dissatisfaction within the medical profession especially. The hardest hit in this field have been the general practitioners whose relationship to their patients is analogous with the relationship between a minister and his

[1] Peter L. Berger, 'Letter on the Parish Ministry', *The Christian Century*, 29th April 1964. Reprinted by permission of the Christian Century Foundation.

parish. The dissatisfaction stems in part from the realization that the general practitioner, like the parson, is dealing with the symptoms rather than the causes of disease, in so far as those causes are located in the major structures of society which are shaping the individual against the grain of his true humanity. The local doctor is as incompetent to deal with these major structures as the local minister.

Berger fully recognizes these limitations and reminds his ordinands that, in spite of them,

you need not come to the conclusion that there is no point to what you are doing *within* people. Even if you deal with individuals rather than with social structures, you will encounter the impact of these structures in each individual life that opens up to you. What is more, if that happens, you will be able to enter into a very rare human relationship—the relationship that occurs between individuals who talk to each other about the ultimate significance of their lives. Quite apart from the theological meaning that this kind of communication will have for you, it is a very privileged one even in purely human terms. Obviously not every minister finds that other lives open up to him in this way. That will to a large extent be up to you; it will depend not so much on what you do as who you are.

For Berger the 'absurdity' of the ministry stems very much from the 'absurdity' of the Christian faith as such. To that extent this absurdity should be the burden of every Christian, not simply of the minister. The difference for the minister, however, lies in the fact that he is a full-time and public embodiment of this absurdity, unlike the rest of the laity who can at any time shelve their 'lay-priestly' role and take refuge, as Berger says, 'in the *weltanschauliche* neutrality of their publicly recognized vocational role'. There is a genuine sense, therefore, in which the minister is expected to fulfil a ministry vicariously on behalf of the laity who can be content with their half-declared faith and their to-be-taken-half-seriously commitments, retreating from faith and commitment, whenever necessary. Berger sees the minister's role as summed up in the figure of the clown:

> If one combines the idea of absurdity with that of vicariousness, he can think here of a striking analogy: that of the clown. This analogy is not an insult to the ministry; on the contrary it points to the profound significance of the clown, who dances through the world, incongruous in the face of the world's seriousness, contradicting all its assumptions—a messenger from another world, in which tears turn to laughter and the walls of man's imprisonment are breached. In this role the clown carries out a vicarious action: it is for *others* that he is clowning. I think that one can speak of the clown, without exaggeration, as a sacerdotal figure. In absurdity and vicariousness the two figures meet. The clown ministers and the minister clowns. The secret of both is the tale of man's redemption.

Support for this view of the Christian's, rather than just the minister's role, comes from as widely disparate sources as Dietrich Bonhoeffer and the American radical theologian, William Hamilton. In an essay on 'The Death of God Theologies Today', Hamilton refers to the Christian as 'the sucker, the fall guy, the jester, the fool for Christ, the one who stands before Pilate and is silent, the one who stands before power and power-structures and laughs'.[2] In his letter of 9th March 1944 Bonhoeffer writes of the quality of *hilaritas* which is the mark of great men. He defines *hilaritas* as 'confidence in their own work, boldness and defiance of the world and of popular opinion, a steadfast certainty that in their own work they are showing the world something *good* (even if the world does not like it), and a high-spirited self-confidence'.[3]

It is all too easy to mention the very obvious lack of *hilaritas* amongst ministers and church people generally. Often this is

---

[2] W. Hamilton (with T. J. J. Altizer), *Radical Theology and the Death of God*, Bobbs-Merrill Press, 1966, p. 50.

[3] Dietrich Bonhoeffer, *op. cit.*, p. 137.

bound up with a feeling that there is little cause for gaiety in a world replete with tragedy and suffering of all kinds. Such a feeling is fostered by the constant admonition of church members to be 'concerned' about good causes of one sort or another. It is now becoming common for Christians of various denominations to use the Quaker term 'a concern' to describe a sense of responsibility for and commitment to some pressing need in the world. The word 'concern' has slightly unfortunate associations, however, in so far as it suggests in a way foreign to the Quaker usage, a dour and joyless assumption of the role of the 'do-gooder'. Part of the clowning function of the minister will be to sit loose to the heavy seriousness of so much 'Christian work'. This is difficult to do in a situation where he is traditionally expected to be the embodiment of altruistic concern. Such concern, however, is often motivated by the desire to manage other people's lives for them, a form of power-seeking every whit as demonic as the 'power-game' played in non-Church circles. I do not wish to decry the Church's practical service of the community where it is a genuine expression of the servanthood of Christ. But service of this kind is markedly different in quality from that which is conducted purely out of a desire to assuage the guilt feelings of the Christian. In my ministry in the East End of London, a traditional hunting ground for the 'do-gooder', I discovered how shrewdly the East Enders could distinguish between genuine service which respected their own integrity as human beings and service based upon the desire to manipulate them.

The difficulties for the minister in the way of sitting loose to the 'principalities and powers' within the Church should not be underestimated. He will find the congregation trying to manipulate him continually back into the role of a sounding board for their own views concerning what it is right and proper for the Christian to feel and do. I have already referred in the Introduction to the intolerable strain placed upon me earlier in my ministry by the attempt to conform to the Church's expectations of me as an upholder of the *status quo*. In the process I found that I was evading the real issue of the Gospel, in so far as I was afraid, as I still am in many ways, to die to other people's expectations of me. The unwillingness to die in this sense precluded any real possibility of discovering my identity as a person in my own right, and thus any possibility of fulfilling my vocation as a minister, which is to teach others how to die. There is indeed a sense in which the minister exists to teach men how to die. His ability to contradict the world's seriousness rests upon the extent to which he has been grasped by the Christian message of death and resurrection. For it is precisely the fear of dying which causes us to cling so frantically to the past and to take refuge from the future. As a result, structures and institutions such as the Church itself become demonic in so far as they thwart men's freedom to face the future free from guilt and fear. The Church, above all, is tempted to take itself far too seriously as a bastion against change and too little seriously as a springboard for change. Like the over-protective mother it tries to prevent its charges from taking the risks which are an inevitable and necessary part of all true growth. Where the Church succumbs to this temptation it becomes a standing denial of the Gospel which it professes, a Gospel concerning the resurrection which is granted to those who have learned how to die.

I am well aware of the possible dangers of this line of argument. Dietrich Bonhoeffer made devastatingly clear in the *Letters and Papers from Prison* how the Church has been forced by the process of secularization to surrender one area of control after another until it now appears to be relevant only to questions concerning the so-called 'last things', particularly death. It is dishonest of the Church to try and whip up in people a concern for the question of death merely in order to justify its existence as the possessor of a supposed answer to that question. But this is not a genuine preaching of the Christian message of resurrection. For this message to become real it must be seen as relevant to the whole of a man's life, not only to its biological termination. The meaning of resurrection for people at every stage of life must be interpreted in terms of the succession of minor deaths which we all undergo as a necessary part of living at all. This is very different from the 'other-worldliness' which Bonhoeffer criticizes. Indeed he writes in one of his letters about living in the light of the resurrection :

Easter? We are paying more attention to dying than to death. We are more concerned to get over the act of dying than to over- come death. Socrates mastered the art of dying; Christ overcame death as 'the last enemy' (I Cor. 15.26). There is a real difference between the two things; the one is within the scope of human possibilities, the other means resurrection. It is not from *ars moriendi*, the art of dying, but from the resurrection of Christ, that a new and purifying wind can blow through our present world. . . . If a few people really believed that and acted on it in their daily lives, a great deal would be changed. To live in the light of the resurrection—that is what Easter means.[4]

Before he can preach this message to others the minister must listen to it himself. The difficulties facing the minister who wishes simply to hear the Gospel of resurrection for himself, let alone embody it, are enormous. One of these difficulties is that created by the many and varied requirements laid upon him by the congregation, as discussed in Chapter 2. One of the most crippling of these requirements is that he should somehow be a figure of strength to those who depend upon him. The tendency for congregations to idealize the minister makes it very difficult for him to admit weakness, either to himself or to others. He will be tempted to find means of bolstering his own image of himself as professionally competent, even at the expense of realism in his dealings with himself, his family and his congre- gation. The myth of the ever available pastoral figure can be

[4] *Op. cit.*, p. 146.

maintained only by the minister who is afraid to die to the identities forced upon him by others. It is impossible, let alone undesirable, for the minister to dart like a hare after every parishioner who claims his time simply to keep his own professional image intact. It is both unrealistic and unloving of the minister to neglect the need for times of withdrawal from his 'pastoral' work in order to relax and recoup his energies. It is unrealistic because it is impossible to be omnipotent. So many ministers are afraid to let go the reins for fear they lose control of the situation or simply because they hate missing anything. In either case the misplaced attempt to control our own destiny as well as that of others is rooted in the sheer unwillingness to die. It is also unloving of the minister not to make himself unavailable at times, because he is liable to be rendered less effective for the task of ministering to those who really need his help. Loving pastoral care must be selective if the minister is to conduct a fruitful ministry of listening as described in Chapter 4.

Another crippling requirement which prevents the minister from hearing and embodying the Gospel of resurrection is the requirement that he should be 'successful'. Such a requirement begs the question of where success in the ministry lies. It is still common for the 'success' of the minister to be judged by the size of his Sunday congregations. My ministry in Stepney to a tiny handful of a congregation had robbed me, so I thought, of any tendency to judge myself in terms of church attendance. However, the fact that in my present church I continue at times to feel guilty about small numbers on occasions indicates the extent to which this false criterion of success still dominates me. In the light of the discussion in Chapter 6 on 'God's Arithmetic' and the representative function of the Church it might appear that the really successful minister would perhaps be distinguished more by his ability to reduce the size of his congregation rather than increase it. But the desire to be successful in the wrong sense takes more subtle forms than simply a concern about numbers. A minister who has been trained in techniques of pastoral counselling, for instance, will certainly face the temptation of expecting success with all his parishioners. The tendency to regard oneself as a kind of expert in human relations must be fought all along the line. In the professional social services high case-loads quickly dispel the feeling in the freshly-trained social worker that there is no problem he can tackle without hope of success. The fact that a minister can often devote more time and attention to an individual sufferer than the professional case-worker can delude him into persisting with an intractable problem beyond the point where any more help can be given. The minister may rightly refuse to let go of a parishioner who has been rejected as hopeless by all the secular social agencies, simply because of his refusal, in the light of the Gospel, to accept any case as hopeless. On the other hand he may fall into the trap of persisting with an unprofitable counselling relationship because he cannot admit to himself that he has failed. The parishioner then becomes not an end in himself but a means to an end, namely the bolstering of the minister's self-esteem.

Such a death to popular ideas of 'strength' and 'success' represent only a fraction of the ways in which a minister is required to die to other people's expectations of him. On the whole he will find that he is struggling continually against the middle-class morality which infects all ecclesiastical institutions. Middle-class values are not to be sneered at; nevertheless, they have a demonic capacity for stifling the authentic note of the Gospel, which is that a man is to be judged less by what he can do and more by what he is in the sight of God. We are brought back here to the proper role of the Christian minister, as discussed in Chapter 1, namely as a person who witnesses to the importance of being rather than doing. This witness is only possible for the minister who has learned to evaluate failure positively in terms of Calvary and Easter. A positive evaluation of failure in these terms is very different from the attitude to failure common amongst ministers. A minister can be as much bemused by wrong ideas of failure as of success. There is a kind of spiritual masochism which makes ministers wallow quite unnecessarily in failure. Our failure to retain professional prestige and status in an age where clergymen in England, at least, have become downgraded socially, can be worn as a badge of the wrong kind. Ministers have become so used to being treated as failures that they can begin all too easily to enjoy the meal of tragedy which tends to be our daily diet. They can even begin to cultivate failure by almost deliberately seeking out situations where they have not the slightest chance of success. This tendency is, of course neurotic and may need to be dealt with by psychological means before it gains a complete hold upon the minister afflicted with it. It is, in fact, merely an inversion of the problem facing the 'success-seeker', in so far as the spiritual masochist wishes, paradoxically, to be a 'successful failure'.

Failure viewed in the light of Calvary and Easter is a healthy phenomenon, in that it runs along the grain of that true wholeness of which Christ is the embodiment. The ability to accept failure is rooted, first and foremost, in the ability to accept oneself which, in its turn, springs from the awareness, however fragmentary, of being accepted by God. I stress the fragmentary nature of this awareness, particularly for the sake of those ministers, probably the majority, who possess highly developed neurotic consciences which continually frustrate the growth of an awareness of God's acceptance of them as they are. An unbroken sense of acceptance is given to very few; indeed the experience of being grasped by it may come only a few times in a whole lifetime. Nevertheless, through the constant re-presentation and *anamnesis* in liturgy and sacrament of the drama of Calvary and Easter a minister is privileged to reappropriate the great facts on which his acceptance by God in Jesus Christ is based. It is a tragedy that the setting for liturgy and sacrament

within the Church as it is has evacuated them of so much of
their force, as I have argued in these pages. All the same, the
Christian who has had even the most fleeting experience of
being accepted by God will respond by celebrating the fact in
one way or another, perhaps without recourse to the traditional
forms of worship or benefit of clergy. The acceptance of failure
in the light of Calvary and Easter means the acceptance of forgiveness. As the full-time embodiment of the reality of forgiveness for the world the minister will be struggling continually
against the heavy associations of guilt and condemnation which
hang around his office. He will tend to be most censorious with
himself and betray that self-loathing which is the antithesis of
the Christian Gospel. If he is married he will tend to make life
difficult for his wife and family, who will be forced to bear the
brunt of most of his unresolved guilt and the depression to which
it gives rise. Such a situation is perhaps hardest for the sensitive
minister to bear. Failure in his public role may be tolerable, but
failure in his private role as husband and father can be crippling.
Yet even this failure, once recognized and accepted, can become
material for the preaching in diverse ways of the 'absurd' message that God can actually use and redeem failure as he has done
at Calvary. I have said little throughout this book of the minister's family life, partly because of the difficulty of speaking
about it with the necessary detachment. I cannot close this book,
however, without mentioning the minister's home as probably
the greatest testing-ground for the foolishness of preaching. It
cannot be over-emphasized that the man who seeks a 'successful'
ministry in the popular sense will be doing so at the expense of
his family. Few congregations realize how much strain their
minister's efforts at omnicompetence place upon his home life.
Ministers' wives on the whole know what it is to be treated by
congregations less as a person in their own right and more as an
appendage to the minister. The minister's dependence upon the
congregation for housing can make it all the more difficult for

him to achieve the self-respect which comes from providing wholly for his family. The nature of ministerial stipends also leaves him little opportunity to accumulate the capital which ensures an easy retirement at the end of his professional career. He must also cope with the sense of insecurity associated, in the Free Churches at least, with the fact that he is dependent financially upon an institution which is fast dwindling in strength economically as well as numerically. I doubt whether the ordinand today will be able to expect a whole lifetime in the professional ministry. His training should certainly prepare him for the probability of a change of career in middle life. Considerations such as these are not the best basis for a stable home life. There is evidence that the brunt of the institutional breakdown within the Church is being borne by ministers' families, in terms of neurosis and accumulated resentment, particularly on the part of the children, against the Church on which they are made to feel so dependent.

Nevertheless, the minister who chooses to continue in the parish ministry will need to accept these limitations honestly, for in the end it is his own attitude towards them which will be determinative for the quality of his home life as of his ministry. The two cannot be separated, for every aspect of the minister's life is grist for the mill where preaching the 'absurd' news of God's love is concerned. The minister who has learned to forgive himself for the failures of his closest personal relationships within the home will be equipped to deal with failure all along the line. For ultimately the ministry begins and ends at the point where this discussion of a 'ministry renewed' was initiated; with the fact that all the minister has to offer the world is his own humanity, broken though it is, a humanity shot through with the awareness that the final word on man's condition is one of acceptance, forgiveness and resurrection :

We have this treasure in earthen vessels, to show that the transcendent power belongs to God and not to us. We are afflicted in every way, but not crushed; perplexed, but not driven to despair; persecuted, but not forsaken; struck down, but not destroyed; always carrying in the body the death of Jesus, so that the life of Jesus may also be manifested in our bodies. For while we live we are always being given up to death for Jesus' sake, so that the life of Jesus may be manifested in our mortal flesh. So death is at work in us, but life in you (II Cor. 4.7-12).